Burnout in Probation and Corrections

BURNOUT IN PROBATION AND CORRECTIONS

JOHN T. WHITEHEAD

PRAEGER

New York
Westport, Connecticut
London

Library of Congress Cataloging-in-Publication Data

Whitehead, John T.
Burnout in probation and corrections / John T. Whitehead.
p. cm.
Bibliography: p.
Includes index.
ISBN 0-275-92959-0 (alk. paper)
1. Probation officers—United States—Job stress. 2. Parole officers—United States—Job stress. 3. Burn out (Psychology) I. Title. II. Title: Burn-out in probation and corrections.
HV9304.W46 1989
364.6'01'9—dc19 88-28776

Library of Congress Catalog Card Number: 88-28776
ISBN: 0-275-92959-0

First published in 1989

Praeger Publishers, One Madison Avenue, New York, NY 10010
A division of Greenwood Press, Inc.

Printed in the United States of America

The paper used in this book complies with the Permanent Paper Standard issued by the National Information Standards Organization (Z39.48--1984).

10 9 8 7 6 5 4 3 2 1

To Pat, Danny, and Timmy

Contents

Tables and Figures

TABLES

FIGURES

Acknowledgments

Writing this book would not have been possible without the assistance of many people.

David Duffee agreed to be my dissertation advisor at SUNY-Albany and thereby took on more work than either of us anticipated. Although this book represents five years of additional research and analysis, his influence persists.

Charles Lindquist was a tireless and enthusiastic collaborator on the research reported in Chapter 10 of this book. Together we accomplished more than we ever expected. Furthermore, without him, there would be far fewer semicolons in this book.

Bob Langworthy and Steve Lab have proven to be cherished friends, inspiring collaborators, and genuine sources of encouragement. Bob specifically urged me to submit the proposal for this book and thus deserves a special note of gratitude.

Two graduate assistants deserve mention. Susan Gunn at the University of Alabama at Birmingham assisted in the qualitative analysis presented in Chapter 9. Ken Pearson at East Tennessee State University assisted in the bibliographic search.

Acknowledgment also needs to be made that several portions of this book originally appeared as journal articles and are now presented in book form with some modifications. Specifically, portions of Chapter 5 on the levels of burnout in the sample first appeared as "Job burnout in probation and parole: Its extent and intervention implications" in *Criminal Justice and Behavior*, Vol. 12, pages 91–110 (1985); adapted and reprinted by permission of Sage Publications, Inc. Article versions of Chapters 6 and 8 originally appeared in the *Journal of Criminal Justice* as "Probation officer job burnout: A test of two theories," Vol. 15, pages 1–16 (1987), and "Job burnout and job satisfaction among probation managers," Vol. 14, pages 25–35 (1986), respectively; adapted and reprinted with permission, Pergamon Press. An earlier version of Chapter 7 appeared as "Gender differences in probation: A case of no differences" in *Justice Quarterly*, Vol. 3, pages 51–64 (1986); adapted and reprinted with permission of the Academy of Criminal Justice Sciences. The path analysis of correctional officer burnout originally appeared as "Correctional officer job burnout: A path analysis" in the *Journal of Research in Crime and Delinquency*, Vol. 23, pages 23–42; coauthored with Charles A. Lindquist and adapted and reprinted by permission of Sage Publications, Inc. Finally, the qualitative analysis of officer comments originally appeared as

"Probation employee job attitudes" in the *Journal of Crime and Justice*, Vol. 10, no. 2, 1987; coauthored with Susan Gunn and adapted and reprinted by permission of Anderson Publishing Co.

Two grants assisted the research. A National Institute of Justice Grant (81-IJ-CX-0039) provided support for much of the data collection for the research reported in this book. A Graduate School Research Grant from the University of Alabama at Birmingham provided support for the collection and analysis of the data on the Alabama employees (see Chapter 10).

Gratitude also needs to be expressed to the approximately 1,500 probation, parole, and prison employees who took the time and trouble to complete questionnaires. Without them, this book would never have become a reality.

Last, but really first, Pat assisted me, supported me emotionally, and gave both of us two sons who make our lives worthwhile even when we start to feel burned out.

Burnout in Probation and Corrections

1 Introduction

In the last 20 years, the problem of job burnout has become a topic of serious concern to students of the human service occupations. In 1969, Bradley noted that writers were beginning to observe "the staff 'burn out' phenomenon in intensive treatment programs" (Bradley, 1969, p. 366). In 1974, Freudenberger saw his fellow free clinic workers beginning to "fail, wear out, or become exhausted by making excessive demands on energy, strength, or resources" (Freudenberger, 1974, p. 159). Maslach and Jackson, defining burnout as a "syndrome of emotional exhaustion and cynicism that occurs frequently among individuals who do 'people-work' of some kind" (1981, p. 1), have studied the problem among such diverse professionals as lawyers, physicians, social workers, psychologists, child-care workers, ministers, and police officers (Maslach, 1976, 1978a, 1978b, 1982; Maslach & Jackson, 1978, 1979, 1981, 1984a, 1984b). Daley (1979), Harrison (1980), and Pines and Kafry (1978) have reported research on the existence and extent of burnout among social workers; Edelwich (1980) has sketched the stages of the burnout process for such workers. Others have examined the problem among police officers (Burke & Deszca, 1986; Burke, Shearer, & Deszca, 1984), Social Security Administration staff (Barad, 1979), school teachers (Blough, 1980, Morgan & Krehbiel, 1985), and human service agency administrators (Vash, 1980). More generally, Cherniss (1980a, 1980b) has argued that the problem is prevalent among "public" professionals, that is, professionals working in bureaucratic organizations, such as poverty lawyers, public school teachers, and public health nurses, as well as among social workers and mental health workers.

In addition to attention in the scholarly literature, the interest in burnout has sparked journalistic accounts of the problem in several occupations (e.g., Bernhard, 1981; Bridgwater, 1984; Johnson, 1984; Kennedy, 1985; Konrad, 1986; Yuenger, 1981), prevention training programs and workshops, and national conferences (Paine, 1982). More mundanely, burnout has grown from its status as a word used to describe one stage of missile launching (Guralnik, 1980) to its current acceptance as a word to describe both an occupational problem and a more generic state of exhaustion.

All of these developments demonstrate the recent interest in burnout in general and two more specific concerns. First, there is concern that dedicated workers may become disillusioned and abandon human service occupations. Second, there is fear that some previously dedicated workers may become exhausted, callous, and cynical but continue in their jobs. In the first adaptation, the worker may well be forsaking what could be a successful career, and the client may be losing the services of a conscientious service provider. In the second adaptation, the worker is insulating him/herself against the potential intrinsic satisfactions of the job, and the client is forced to deal with a cold bureaucrat. But burnout may have positive consequences. A worker who has weathered the storm of burnout and managed to cope in a positive manner may be a more competent professional. Alternatively, the experience of burnout may influence an individual who is not suited for human service work to leave the field and thus benefit both that individual and clients (Daley, 1979).

Based on this interest in the occupational problems of workers in the human services, this book explores the nature and extent of burnout in probation and parole officers and in correctional officers. A standardized burnout instrument, the Maslach Burnout Inventory (Maslach & Jackson, 1981), was administered to a sample of probation and parole officers in the Northeast; later, a modified version of the instrument, the Human Services Inventory, was administered to a sample of correctional officers and a sample of probation and parole officers in Alabama. Also included in the questionnaires were measures of job satisfaction, role conflict, and demographic variables.

Much of this research has been reported in several scholarly journals (Whitehead, 1985, 1986a, 1986b, 1987; Whitehead & Lindquist, 1985, 1986). This book represents a more complete account of that research, new information not previously published, and a chance to synthesize all the research and to extract the full implications of the research. It is hoped that this compilation will prove helpful to other researchers on job burnout who have not seen all the earlier reports. Likewise, it is hoped that this book will be helpful to criminal justice professionals who lack easy access to scholarly journals. Finally, the book should be of interest to criminal justice students who are contemplating careers in probation, parole, or other types of correctional programs because burnout can be a problem in those occupations.

RESEARCH RATIONALE

This exploration of the problem of burnout in corrections seems justified on several grounds. First and most directly, it can clarify the nature and extent of the problem of burnout as it confronts correctional personnel. Impressionistic accounts clearly suggest that burnout is a problem in the field. Shireman and Reamer (1986), for example, contend that the following scenario is typical for correctional employees who work with juvenile delinquents:

> Programs for this population [juvenile delinquents] are frequently staffed by persons who, if they were not hardened and cynical upon their induction into the profession, quickly become so. The scenario frequently unfolds thusly: relatively young, eager faces, fresh with idealism, are attracted to correctional programs because of a sincere

> belief that what misguided youths need is a fair shake in life and decent, respectful, and empathic care. With refreshing enthusiasm that the naivete of inexperience fosters, these young professionals charge into a system rife with stagnation, punitiveness, indifference, cynicism, inconsistency, and disingenuousness. True commitment to the values that drive nascent professionals is hard to locate, they discover, and where it can be found it is often camouflaged by pernicious views and policies. Those who do not flee the field quickly become "realists," whose agendas are quickly revised in light of the resistance they face. Though they may not abandon their commitment entirely, their zeal is diluted. There are those, of course, who manage to sustain their devotion to the rehabilitative ideal despite the obstacles on the way, but their numbers are small when placed in the context of the formal juvenile justice system (police, courts, correctional programs) that surrounds them (pp. 167–68).

Likewise, Clear (1985), citing Lipsky (1980), has argued that burnout is a frequent problem in probation and parole: "in most organizations, probation is seen as an early-career position which most people eventually leave to take other jobs. Few people stay in community corrections work for their entire professional careers. . . . Turnover is often high, 'burnout' is epidemic and work world cynicism seems to pervade the office" (p. 40).

This research seeks to document and clarify such impressionistic accounts. Clarification is important because correctional employees face problems that are similar to the problems in other human service fields yet unique to probation, parole, and prisons. Unlike the lawyers studied by Cherniss (1980a), for example, probation, parole, and correctional officers confront the problem of working in a correctional system that has been criticized by many for being ineffective (see Cullen & Gilbert, 1982; Sechrest, White, & Brown, 1979, for reviews of this issue). A second example of problems unique to probation, parole, and correctional officers is the problem of dealing with reluctant, and perhaps alienated, clients. Many other agencies can choose their clientele, but criminal justice agencies usually have no choice. Likewise, the clients usually have no choice regarding their wish to be served or which worker in the agency will serve them. This problem was mentioned in the pioneering work of Ohlin, Piven, and Pappenfort (1956) who noted that a conflict often exists between probation officers with social work backgrounds, who have an orientation to professional social work service, and the agency, with its orientation to public safety and efficiency. This work will apply the conceptual framework of burnout to criminal justice personnel to compare their occupational problems with problems of their counterparts in other human service occupations.

Second, the study of burnout can aid probationers, parolees, and prisoners if ways can be devised to alleviate the work pressures of those who serve them. Waller (1974), for example, has contended that Canadian parole workers often became mere dictators of case records, rather than innovative problem solvers for socially detached parolees. Likewise, before the popularity of the notion of burnout, Studt (1973) noted that most California parole officers "mellowed" but that a few unfortunately became disillusioned and left the field (Studt, 1973, p. 54). Thus two respected studies of parole have hinted at the problem of job burnout, but neither study concentrated on the problem directly to clarify its extent or to suggest solutions. Here it is hoped, at least, to clarify the problem so that work can begin on the solution.

Third, the research can be of assistance in the current policy debate about the mission of community supervision. Some (e.g., Dietrich, 1979) continue to emphasize a focus on offender needs; some (e.g., Conrad, 1973, 1982, 1984) call for an emphasis on offender surveillance; and some call for new conceptualizations that integrate past models or go beyond previous models to focus on justice (Fogel, McAnany, & Thomson, 1980), public safety (Fogel, 1984), or risk control (Clear & O'Leary, 1983; O'Leary & Clear, 1984). This rethinking of the mission of probation and parole is occurring because there is new concern about the amount of crime committed by offenders under supervision in the community (Petersilia, Turner, Kahan, & Paterson, 1985). Research on the job problems of officers is critical in any consideration of mission reform because line officers are the ones who actually translate policy into practice (McCleary, 1978).

Finally, there seems to be a need to place this current concern on burnout within the broader context of the research on the occupational problems of workers in general and of probation, parole, and correctional officers in particular. As Sarason has remarked in the foreword to one of Cherniss's books:

> Reading the literature, scholarly and popular, one might gain the impression that we are dealing with a new phenomenon, although a little reflection would suggest that that is not likely to be the case. It is like "discovering" the problems of aging, as if they were newly minted by contemporary society (cited in Cherniss, 1980a, p. vii).

If the current concern with burnout is placed in the context of previous research on the occupational problems of probation and parole officers, a broader perspective can be achieved. Problems that appear to be contemporary crises can be viewed more objectively when seen in the light of earlier adjustments of solutions. More fully, it may be that burnout is a new adaptation to old pressures. Now, however, individuals may be responding to rather long-standing problems by the exhaustion, cynicism, and withdrawal that are described as burnout. Furthermore, the workers may be responding in this way because administrators, legislators, and society in general may be unresponsive to perennial problems of the field.

THE OCCUPATIONAL PROBLEMS OF PROBATION AND PAROLE OFFICERS

Having noted the recent concern with the problem of burnout in human service workers in general and having set forth some of the reasons for exploring this topic among probation and parole officers, it is necessary to review the literature on the occupational problems of these workers. One interest is to see the extent to which the problem of burnout has been addressed previously, even if in adumbrated fashion. Such foreshadowings of the current concern may be helpful in clarifying the analysis of the current data.

In their examination of some of the dilemmas facing the social work professional in probation and parole work, Ohlin and his colleagues emphasized the possibility of a conflict between the treatment emphasis learned in graduate school and the social control emphasis of the agency. What is noteworthy about their article in terms of the current concern with burnout is that these authors, writing some 30 years ago, noted the possibility that social workers in probation might

> give up social work entirely disillusioned and convinced that (both) social work as a discipline and corrections as an area of practice are without genuine reward or meaning. Some return to more traditional casework settings, convinced that it is not possible, at least for them, to operate professionally in probation-parole work. Others remain in corrections, unhappy with the most recent job experience (Ohlin et al., 1956, p. 222).

Such disillusionment is a central concern of many writers on burnout (e.g., Edelwich, 1980), as is the issue of leaving the field (Harrison, 1980). Likewise, the problem of the individual worker's striving for professionalism is an important element in Cherniss's (1980a, 1980b) writing on the problem of burnout. What is most important to note here is that Ohlin and his colleagues were addressing the issues of frustration and possible disillusionment, although they, of course, never used the term "burnout."

In studying more than 500 federal probation and parole officers, Glaser (1969) discussed some of their occupational problems such as role conflict. Specifically, Glaser delineated the adaptive style an officer might choose in deciding whether to be more or less concerned with the welfare of the probationer versus the protection of the community. Of relevance to the discussion of burnout is one of the styles identified by Glaser, the passive officer who had minimal concern for both the probationer's welfare and the protection of the community. One might read the term burnout into Glaser's description of these passive officers, the political opportunists, who "treat their jobs as sinecures which require only minimum efforts" (Glaser, 1969, p. 293). Such "minimum efforts" parallel the depersonalization (Maslach, 1976) and overdetachment (Cherniss, 1980a) described by current writers on burnout who note that once dedicated workers may cope with job stress by limiting their contacts with clients; these contacts may be a key source of stress. The burnout writers posit some initial dedication or commitment to the job (e.g., Freudenberger, 1974) whereas Glaser said the passive officers earned their appointments as officers through political patronage for past political favors and were not necessarily interested in the job as an opportunity to perform dedicated service. Thus, Glaser's description of one type of officer appears very similar to recent descriptions of the burned out worker, but the process leading to that end state may have been very different.

In the same vein, Klockars labeled some officers "time-servers": "that category of probation officers who find no law-enforcing or casework vocation in probation. Instead, they see their jobs as having certain requirements to be fulfilled until their retirement. . . . Their conduct on the job is rule-abiding and their job responsibilities are met minimally but methodically" (Klockars, 1976, p. 404). If these time-servers began as dedicated workers and became time-servers as a result of a coping reaction to stress in the job, then they burned out in the current sense of the term. If, however, they started out as time-servers or "clock-watchers," then they cannot be said to have burned out. The initial dedication may have been in a job other than probation; an officer may have started in a welfare agency, for example, and then transferred to probation, but the worker must have been dedicated at one time.

Elliot Studt (1973) seems to have come the closest to being a precursor of the recent writers on burnout. First, she noted some of the "strains" confronting parole officers such as the problem of competence; agents "are expected to be expert in a vast range of human problem situations far beyond the possibilities of individual competence" (Studt, 1973, p. 50). Also many problems of parolees are practical or economic such as the need for reentry funds or the need for job training, yet the parole agents lack the technology to solve these problems. In the context of burnout, Cherniss (1980a, 1980b) has claimed that human service workers seek a sense of efficacy but that they experience the "myth of professional competence," that academic credentials automatically prepare new workers to begin practice in an effective manner. This myth ignores the need for practical experience and the fact that clients often have difficult, if not intractable, problems (Cherniss, 1980a). Studt (1973) mentioned other strains such as the problem of the seduction to power, which refers to the agent's power to initiate a return to prison for the parolee and thereby perform a fate-determining role in the parolee's life. The problem with the seduction to power lies in the possibility of threatening or manipulating parolees who cannot really complain about such actions. All this leads to tension, as indicated by officers' jokes about "playing God" (Studt, 1973, p. 49).

Studt (1973) argued that parole officers adjust to the strains of parole work in a four-step process: naive idealism, "toughening-up," "mellowing," and disillusionment. This process is very similar to the burnout process; that is, Studt was describing the same stress-coping process that burnout writers are analyzing (Cherniss, 1980a, 1980b; Edelwich, 1980; Maslach, 1982). What is different in Studt's depiction is that she concluded that most agents progressed to stage three, mellowing, in which they see parolees as fellow human beings who make mistakes and can benefit from leniency in cases of minor rule breaking. She said only "occasional" agents reach the fourth stage of disillusionment or remain fixed in the second stage of cynicism toward clients (Studt, 1973, p. 54) whereas the burnout writers imply that the problem occurs more frequently. One questions, therefore, whether these recent claims about the prevalence of the problem are also true of probation and parole officers or whether Studt's (1973) estimate of the extent of the problem in parole is still accurate.

In attempting to clarify the factors influencing recidivism, Waller (1974) tangentially touched on the issue of burnout among parole officers. Specifically, Waller claimed that a major problem among Canadian parole officers was the presence of agents "who remain detached from the parolee in a personal sense, but who continue to fulfill job requirements by using the dictaphone and recording man-hours supervised" (Waller, 1974, p. 211). If these officers were once dedicated workers, one could conclude that they had burned out. An alternative explanation is that these officers always had been so detached from their clients.

Based on 20 years of observation in "Metropolitan Court," Blumberg (1979) wrote a diatribe on what he considered the civil service "malaise" of probation officers. According to Blumberg, officers are individuals who have changed their career sights from professional social work or some other low-paying job to the court-dominated bureaucracy of probation for the sake of an attractive pay scale and civil service security. The pay and the security compensate for the lack of professionalism in the job but lead to some negative outcomes: "Frustrated as professionals, stripped of real decision-making power, lacking a genuine career motif, and assigned relatively low status by the community, it is not surprising that probation workers often develop a high degree of cynicism" (Blumberg, 1979, p. 283). This cynicism is compounded by misanthropy in order to avoid being deceived by administrators or clients. Finally, "occupational voyeurism," the observing and prying into the sordid details of clients' lives, relieves to some extent "the drabness and monotony of probation work" (Blumberg, 1979, p. 284). In summary, Blumberg concluded that the lack of promotional opportunities and the lack of true professionalism promote the "malaise" that others might label "bureaucracy" in all the negative connotations of that word. As was mentioned earlier and will be expanded later, Cherniss (1980a) has emphasized some of these same bureaucratic constraints as potential causes of burnout.

After conducting interviews and participant observation with a small sample of parole officers, McCleary (1978) painted a portrait that can be interpreted in two ways. On the one hand, one might say that the officers McCleary studied burned out because they started out idealistically but quickly became bureaucrats in the pejorative sense of that term; they quickly learned that the agency is most interested in protecting and maintaining itself and that the parolees often prefer to avoid officers rather than to seek them out as counselors. This, the reading that McCleary himself took, is congruent with descriptions of burnout as a process of distancing oneself from clients and becoming disillusioned with initial ideals (see, e.g., Edelwich, 1980). However, a more critical reading of McCleary shows that the officers he studied valued graduate education in counseling and tried to incorporate the counseling role into their jobs. Some even conducted group sessions for some of the parolees on their caseloads (McCleary, 1978, p. 170). Thus, one could argue that these officers were not burning out but were actively attempting to solve the problems they were encountering on the job. As Cherniss (1980a) has pointed out, such problem solving is very different from the defensive coping of withdrawing from client contact, that is, from the process of burnout.

In a humorous look at the occupational problems of probation officers, Erickson (1977, 1978, 1980), the probation version of Erma Bombeck, poked fun at the day-to-day difficulties of officers: increasing caseloads, high expectations, scarce resources, and idealistic training. Erickson also noted a frequent adaptation to job pressures: flight to the coffee room or to field visits. In short, Erickson etched a humorous depiction of both the symptoms and the adaptations to what is now being labeled burnout.

Thomson and Fogel (1980) recently surveyed probation in small agencies (fewer than ten officers) concerning perceived training needs. Although burnout was not explicitly mentioned in the report, several of the problem areas cited by the officers, for example, caseload size and an overemphasis on paperwork, relate to what Cherniss (1980a, 1980b), Maslach (1982), and others have listed as causal factors of burnout.

Although he did not explicitly address the issue of burnout, Polisky (1981a, 1981b) found that degree of participatory management, clarity of expectations, the setting of attainable goals, the offering of support and feedback, and the need for upward mobility were all related to job satisfaction for probation officers. As will be shown, several writers on burnout have related these variables to the prevalence of burnout.

Several articles in *Federal Probation*, the journal read by more probation and parole officers than any other, have dealt with burnout (see, e.g., Brown, 1986, 1987; Smith, 1982). All, however, were descriptive or impressionistic accounts, rather than reports of original research.

Textbooks on corrections in general and probation and parole in particular have touched on burnout directly or indirectly through a discussion of the occupational problems of the officer. Interestingly, Trester (1981) wrote of burned out judges (those who became callous and nonobjective) (Trester, 1981, p. 27), but not of burned out probation or parole officers even though he described their problems of a poor image, unwilling clients, and oversized caseloads (Trester, 1981, p. 285). Hussey and Duffee noted that several issues face the field officer, including choice of intervention style, low pay, negative self-image, and agency-precipitated officer-client conflict (Hussey & Duffee, 1980, pp. 301–6). Burnout itself, however, was not mentioned as a problem. Keve, apparently an optimist, ignored any discussion of burnout or other negative issues; for him the probation "field as a whole is dynamic, changing, and capable of much new growth as it seeks to keep its function and identity in tune with current needs" (Keve, 1981, p. 285). Others (Shover & Einstadter, 1988; Symkla, 1984) have referred to some of the research that has been conducted on burnout in criminal justice settings. Finally, Bartollas (1981) noted the causes of burnout in probation work — large caseloads, low pay, little training, and inadequate community resources, but he was convinced that successful officers can avoid burnout:

> through self-awareness, they learn to keep their personal problems separate from their clients' problems. Most importantly, they are

> committed to their jobs, not just to a paycheck. Their motivation remains constant and strengthens them against burnout. Many remain as involved in their work as they were on their first day on the job (Bartollas, 1981, p.155).

For Bartollas, then, the prevention of burnout is a matter of individual effort warding off the problems imposed by clients or the organization.

BURNOUT AMONG CORRECTIONAL OFFICERS

Recent writing on correctional officers has examined several job problems among correctional officers (prison guards), including alienation (Toch & Klofas, 1982), burnout (Schlacter, 1980; Lindquist & Whitehead, 1986a; Whitehead & Lindquist, 1986), cynicism (Farmer, 1977), job dissatisfaction (Jacobs, 1978; Lombardo, 1981), occupational tedium (Shamir & Drory, 1982), and job stress (Cheek & Miller, 1983; Cullen, Link, Wolfe, & Frank, 1985; Johnson, 1977; Long, Shouksmith, Voges, & Roache, 1986). (For reviews of the literature on correctional officer job problems, see Johnson, 1987; Philiber, 1987.) As was the case with much of the research on police officer stress (Cullen, Link, Travis, & Lemming, 1983; Kroes, Margolis, & Hurrell, 1974; Malloy & Mays, 1984), much of this research has found that administrative problems such as lack of officer participation in decision making and lack of administrative support for line officers are more stressful for officers than problems arising from interaction with inmates.

One report has taken the position that burnout is not really a problem for correctional officers although alienation is (Toch & Klofas, 1982). It seems important, however, to examine the issue of possible burnout among correctional officers more carefully. What is particularly important is an examination of the sources of burnout among correctional officers because only a few studies (e.g., Dignam, Barrera, & West, 1986; Shamir & Drory, 1982) have used a multivariate analysis to assess empirically the contribution of various hypothesized sources of job burnout. Hence, this report offers data on both the extent and sources of job burnout in a sample of correctional officers.

SUMMARY

Burnout has become a matter of important concern to human service professionals, as evidenced by the burgeoning literature on the topic. Although criminal justice researchers have lagged behind, they too have begun to devote increasing attention to the problem of burnout in criminal justice settings. This increasing attention is justified because previous writing on probation, parole, and prison personnel has indicated that definite problems in the field can lead to burnout.

What is needed next is a clear description of burnout. Chapter 2, therefore, clarifies the concept of burnout by reviewing various definitions of the phenomenon.

The Conceptualization of Burnout 2

The interest in job burnout noted in Chapter 1 has resulted in a variety of definitions of the problem rather than a consensus. This, however, should not be surprising; the term has been in use for only about 20 years.

This chapter will review some of the pioneering definitions of burnout. The review will show important variations in the conceptualization of burnout, but a common core emerges from a careful examination of the pioneering literature on the phenomenon.

The last section of the chapter analyzes distinctions between burnout and related concepts such as reality shock, alienation, job dissatisfaction, and job stress. These distinctions are important because they show the relationship of the concept of job burnout to much of the previous research on job-related problems.

PIONEERING DEFINITIONS OF BURNOUT

In 1974, Herbert Freudenberger wrote a ground-breaking article in which he presented a dictionary definition of burnout: "to fail, wear out, or become exhausted by making excessive demands on energy, strength, or resources" (Freudenberger, 1974, p. 159). In his experience as a director of a free clinic, Freudenberger noticed that many workers burn out or become inoperative after about one year, often following "the loss of charisma of the leader, and the letdown of the clinic with this disappointment" (Freudenberger, 1974, p. 160). Burned out workers exhibit either irritability, high emotions, and risk taking in counseling or rigidity, cynicism, and depression. Previously dedicated workers spend more time at work but accomplish less. Another aspect of the problem is boredom with the routine of dealing with clients with very similar problems that require repetitious approaches. Finally, probably as a result of his clinical psychology training, Freudenberger postulated that burnout is related to the loss of one's ideals and thus entails a grief experience, including anger "which is always present after grief" (Freudenberger, 1974, p. 165).

Later Freudenberger broadened his depiction and defined burnout as a chronic condition of "someone in a state of fatigue or frustration brought about by devotion to a cause, way of life, or relationship that failed to produce the expected reward" (Freudenberger, 1980, p. 13). The emphasis is shifted from excessive demands in a human service occupation to exhausting oneself "by excessively striving to reach some unrealistic expectation imposed by oneself or by the values of society" (Freudenberger, 1980, p. 16). Such concern for unrealistic expectations can affect anyone, not just helping professionals. Helping professionals, however, are especially prone to burnout because they often are young and idealistic individuals who hope to make an impact on the world but face terrible odds in the workplace: "The people they're trying to help are likely to have surrounded themselves with impenetrable walls. The disappointments mount up until eventually the helpers build walls of their own" (Freudenberger, 1980, p. 12). Freudenberger's prescription for this ailment is to reduce expectations and to strive for self-awareness, a sense of balance in one's life, and intimacy while avoiding false cures such as drugs or compulsive sex (Freudenberger, 1980).

In his most recent discussion of burnout, Freudenberger (1986) has continued to see the problem as a possibility in many sorts of endeavors, not only in human service occupations.

> Burnout is a process that comes about as a consequence of a depletion of energies, as well as feelings of being overwhelmed with many issues that may confront an individual. It is the result of a person's sense of dedication and commitment to a task or job, coupled with a need to prove oneself. In time, it impacts on a person's attitudes, perceptions and judgment (Freudenberger, 1986, p. 247).

Research psychologist Christina Maslach and her associates have also defined burnout, conducted extensive empirical research on the extent and sources of burnout, and produced the leading instrument for measuring the phenomenon, the Human Services Inventory (formerly the Maslach Burnout Inventory). After studying workers in numerous human service occupations, Maslach and Jackson have defined burnout as "a syndrome of emotional exhaustion and cynicism that occurs frequently among individuals who do 'people-work' of some kind" (Maslach & Jackson, 1981, p. 1). More completely, burnout is "the gradual loss of caring about the people they work with. Over time they find that they simply cannot sustain the kind of personal care and commitment called for in the personal encounters that are the essence of their job. And they begin to talk about emotional exhaustion" (Maslach, 1978a, p. 56). Maslach sees burnout as a failure to cope successfully with the chronic stress of client contact. Such contact is stressful because it centers on emotionally charged problems that often are very difficult or impossible to solve. In probation work, for example, a probationer may lack a high school education, marketable job skills, and work experience, have a history of drug or alcohol abuse, and yet expect the probation officer to "find me a job." Such situations can lead to frustration and burnout.

Maslach and Jackson identify three aspects or dimensions of burnout: emotional exhaustion, depersonalization, and lack of personal accomplishment. Exhaustion refers to the situation where workers become worn out and are unable to give of themselves on a psychological level. Depersonalization means that workers develop negative, cynical attitudes and feelings toward clients, possibly even to the extent that workers see clients as deserving their problems (a "blame the victim" philosophy). Lack of personal accomplishment is the tendency of workers to evaluate their work negatively; they feel that they are not achieving their objectives (Maslach & Jackson, 1981).

The notion of three aspects or dimensions of burnout has led Maslach and Jackson to emphasize the complexity of the concept because "conditions and reactions associated with one aspect of burnout are not necessarily associated with other aspects" (Maslach & Jackson, 1984a, pp. 143–44). Because of this complexity, "both researchers and practitioners should avoid conceptualizing burnout as a unitary concept. Instead, they should respect the variety of psychological reactions to a job that employees can experience" (Maslach & Jackson, 1984a, p. 145).

In summary, Maslach emphasizes that the chronic stress of client contact can lead to exhaustion and emotional distancing from clients. Such distancing can manifest itself in retreats to the coffee room or to objectifying clients (treating "cases" rather than human persons), intellectualizing client problems, trying to leave one's job concerns solely at the office, or becoming a mechanical bureaucrat who goes strictly by the book (Maslach, 1976).

Pines and Kafry, two associates of Maslach, have described the problem of burnout as one of occupational tedium that is a pervasive experience of exhaustion

> characterized by feelings of strain and "burnout," by emotional as well as physical depletion, and by negation of one's self and one's environment. It is the experience of distress and discontent with one's work and way of life, the sense of failure, and the feeling that one cannot take it any more (Pines & Kafry, 1978, p. 499).

This notion of tedium is based on research on stress in general, job stress, job satisfaction, and job burnout (see also Pines & Aronson, 1981).

These writers have noted that human service work is asymmetric; the worker primarily gives and the client primarily receives. Furthermore, the personal attributes that attract individuals to the human service professions — a liking for people, rather than things, sympathy, understanding — are the very "attributes that make them more sensitive to the many emotional pressures involved in that work" (Pines & Kafry, 1978, p. 500). Finally, the professional often views failure with a client as personal failure because the key tool in the occupation is the individual worker (Pines & Kafry, 1978).

Given the professional association of Pines and Kafry with Maslach and her other colleagues, it is not surprising that the notion of tedium is very similar to Maslach's conceptualization of burnout. In both cases, the writers view stress in the human service job building to a breaking point where coping is no longer successful: "When work demands exceed one's endurance and ability to cope, when one can no longer tolerate the occupational pressures and feels totally overwhelmed by work stresses, one is likely to reach a breaking point and experience a cluster of symptoms termed 'tedium'" (Pines & Kafry, 1978, p. 499).

Although not colleagues of Maslach, Golembiewski, Munzenrider, and Stevenson (1986) have used the Maslach Burnout Inventory to assess burnout and have claimed that the measure produces scores for nine phases of burnout. (See also Golembiewski & Munzenrider, 1984; Golembiewski, Munzenrider, & Carter, 1983; Golembiewski & Roundtree, 1986.) Basically, the idea is that a person can be high or low on each of the three aspects of burnout. Scoring a person high or low on each dimension gives nine separate scores, which Golembiewski and his colleagues term phases because they find that the scores follow a pattern. Rather than a new definition of burnout these authors offer a refinement of the Maslach and Jackson conceptualization of three aspects of burnout into a nine-phase model of the burnout process.

A different definition of burnout has stemmed from social psychological research conducted at the University of Michigan on job stress, role ambiguity, and role conflict. Specifically, incompatible demands at work, qualitative overload (tasks too difficult to be done satisfactorily), and quantitative overload (too many things to accomplish) can lead to burnout defined as "a syndrome of inappropriate attitudes towards clients and towards self, often associated with uncomfortable physical and emotional symptoms ranging from exhaustion and insomnia to migraine and ulcer. Deterioration of performance is a frequent additional element in the syndrome" (Kahn, 1978, p. 61). Kahn has suggested the following remedies for the problem: improved selection and training, decreasing one's direct contact with clients, and increasing one's social support on the job. Although Kahn's definition is brief, his linking of the concept of burnout to the job stress research merits further consideration, and the latter part of this chapter focuses on distinguishing job burnout from job stress and other problems.

Another definition relating burnout to job stress is Daley's description of the problem as "a reaction to job-related stress that varies in nature with the intensity and duration of the stress itself. It may be manifested in workers becoming emotionally detached from their jobs and may ultimately lead them to leave their job altogether" (Daley, 1979, p. 375). Daley emphasizes that burnout is a dynamic process and that the process can have positive or negative consequences. The experience can be positive if it weeds out workers who made an erroneous career choice or if workers stay in social work but switch to less stressful administrative posts or adjust to the stress. Burnout can be negative, however, if workers who made the wrong career choice stay in the field or if workers who made the right choice adapt by becoming inflexible, cynical bureaucrats.

Daley differs from Maslach in that he sees the causes of burnout being broader than client contact. Writing specifically about child protection workers, Daley notes that they spend at most 25 percent of their time in direct contact with clients; paperwork, meetings, and other tasks fill the rest of the day. Likewise, large caseloads contribute to the frustration of being unable to complete a job, let alone complete it well. Finally, role conflict is a fact of everyday life in protective services; workers constantly face conflicting demands from supervisors, the courts, clients, the community, and other agencies. These demands translate into multiple roles for child protection workers, two of which, therapist and investigator, are contradictory. Daley's comments are especially relevant for probation and parole personnel who face many of the same sources of burnout as child protection workers.

Also writing out of a social work perspective, Edelwich has described burnout as a four-stage process of disillusionment: "a progressive loss of idealism, energy, and purpose experienced by people in the helping professions as a result of the conditions of their work" (Edelwich, 1980, pp. 28–29). The first stage of the process, enthusiasm, is marked by high hopes and unrealistic expectations where the job seems to offer all that one needs in life. The consequent dangers at this stage are "overidentification with clients and excessive and inefficient expenditure of one's energy" (Edelwich, 1980, p. 28). The second stage, stagnation, is characterized by the dawning awareness that overemphasis on the job can lead to neglect of personal needs; the worker feels that he/she is missing out on other satisfactions in life. The third stage, frustration, represents the core of burnout; it leads the professional to begin to question one's effectiveness and the value of the job itself. Apathy, stage four, is the defense mechanism often used to cope with frustration, especially if the worker needs the job to survive and be secure.

Another writer with a social work background has defined burnout rather vaguely as "negative feelings about the work itself" (Harrison, 1980, p. 42). Harrison has operationalized the concept of burnout as job dissatisfaction as measured by the Job Descriptive Index (Hackman & Oldham, 1974), although he has stated that burnout "may not be identical with the more conventional construct, job dissatisfaction" (Harrison, 1980, p. 31). His justification for this somewhat confusing approach is that the Job Descriptive Index is an existing measure of proven validity and reliability. Harrison actually seems to be especially concerned about what the job satisfaction literature calls intrinsic job satisfaction: the worker's attitudes toward the job as opposed to extrinsic satisfaction, attitudes toward such matters as pay and working conditions. If intrinsic satisfaction is lacking burnout can follow:

> These feelings [of burnout] can occur in large part because the work does not encourage or allow for the worker's psychological growth, a feature on which many social workers undoubtedly place a high value. . . . It is argued here that child protection service workers are able to develop positive affective responses to their jobs only if there is some certainty that what they do is valuable and makes a difference in the lives of their clients (Harrison, 1980, p. 42).

Another definition of burnout linking burnout to stress is that offered by Shannon and Saleebey: "Burnout is defined . . . as a debilitating psychological condition afflicting individuals who work in high stress (often human service) jobs brought on probably by the cumulative effects of stress" (1980, p. 463). The symptoms are very similar to those of Maslach: "apathy, negativism, hostility toward clients and agency, emotional distancing from client problems and job context, lack of attentiveness, cynicism, and a decrease in energy and motivation (Shannon & Saleebey, 1980, p. 436).

One of the most comprehensive definitions of burnout is Cary Cherniss's (1980a, 1980b) analysis of burnout as a three-stage process:

> The first stage involves an imbalance between resources and demand (stress). The second stage is the immediate, short-term emotional tension, fatigue, and exhaustion (strain). The third stage consists of a number of changes in attitude and behavior, such as a tendency to treat clients in a detached and mechanical fashion or a cynical preoccupation with gratification of one's own needs (defensive coping). Burnout thus refers to a transactional process, a process consisting of job stress, work strain, and psychological accommodation. Specifically, burnout can now be defined as a process in which a previously committed professional disengages from his or her work in response to stress and strain experienced in the job (Cherniss, 1980b, pp. 17–18).

Several points in Cherniss's analysis are important. First, stage one involving an imbalance between resources and demands can mean excessive demands such as the stress of client contact mentioned by Maslach. Interestingly, however, it can also refer to a state of not enough demands on the worker who, therefore, feels a lack of challenge or stimulation. Second, Cherniss assumes that workers who burn out began their careers as dedicated professionals; thus, burnout turns what was formerly a "calling" into "merely a job" (Cherniss, 1980a, p. 206; 1980b, p. 16). Third, some of the changes associated with burnout may be desirable, unless they go too far. For example, tempering unrealistic or naive expectations and getting involved in extrawork activities are positive adjustments for new human service workers.

Cherniss (1985) appears to be sticking to this depiction of burnout in his more recent writing, and he also emphasizes that perceived helplessness and lack of control are critical aspects of the problem:

> The psychological withdrawal characteristic of burnout occurs when the individual comes to believe that significant work-related stresses are out of his or her control. Problems that can be solved, barriers that can be overcome, do not lead to burnout. In fact, the controllable stresses can have positive effects, stimulating the individual to creative efforts and culminating in gratifying experiences of mastery and competence. But when the individual feels helpless to change the situation, burnout becomes more likely (Cherniss, 1985, p. 48).

SUMMARY OF DEFINITIONS

This review of the definitions of burnout can be synthesized in several conclusions. First, burnout is a process rather than a static condition

(Cherniss, 1980a, 1980b, 1985; Edelwich, 1980; Maslach, 1976, 1982). Workers may be at different stages of the process; they may be just beginning to burn out or may have progressed to more advanced stages. Second, most of the writers agree that burnout is a process of response to chronic and significant stress (Cherniss, 1980a, 1980b, 1985; Maslach, 1976, 1982; Kahn, 1978). Complete understanding of job burnout therefore requires an examination of stress, which will be done in the next section of this chapter. Third, burnout writers assume or have concluded that workers subject to burnout begin their careers with idealistic dedication to human service (Cherniss, 1980a, 1980b; Freudenberger, 1986). Absent such commitment, they could not burn out since burnout implies a transition or transformation. Fourth, there are some differences in conceptualization. Freudenberger (1980) emphasizes that burnout arises from excessive striving to meet unrealistic expectations; this situation can apply to individuals in all sorts of career or personal endeavors, including the young artist who is striving to be another Picasso. Most of the writers on burnout, however, limit the phenomenon to human service workers (Cherniss, 1980a, 1980b; Maslach, 1976, 1982). Another difference in the conceptualizations of burnout is that some writers emphasize unique points. Daley, for example, emphasizes that burnout may be functional in weeding out workers who may have made an incorrect career choice and would be happier in other endeavors (Daley, 1979). Cherniss (1980a, 1980b) makes the important contribution that a lack of demands may be just as stressful for some workers as overload is for others. In conclusion, the writers discussed in this chapter are in fundamental agreement on important aspects of the conceptualization of burnout (for the view that there is considerable lack of consensus concerning a definition of burnout, see Blostein, Eldridge, Kilty & Richardson, 1985), but there are some unique emphases.

BURNOUT AND RELATED CONCEPTS

To complete the analysis of the conceptualization of job burnout, it is necessary to distinguish burnout from several other concepts that might be confused with burnout. Such concepts may be part of the burnout process, but they are not synonyms for burnout. Unfortunately, some writers have confused the conceptualization of burnout by equating it with one of these concepts. The more comprehensive conceptualizations of burnout, such as that of Cherniss (1980a, 1980b), however, explain the precise part these concepts play in the burnout process without confusing such concepts with the larger process of burnout.

Comparison of Burnout and Reality Shock

One term that might be confused with burnout is reality shock. This term has been used in research on civil service workers (Blau, 1974), nurses (Kramer, 1974), and probation and parole officers (Ohlin, Piven, & Pappenfort, 1956). Of these studies, Kramer's thorough investigation of reality shock among nurses offers this definition of the problem:

> the phenomenon and the specific shocklike reactions of new workers when they find themselves in a work situation for which they have spent several years preparing and for which they thought they were going to be prepared, and then suddenly find that they are not. The concept as used in this book will focus mainly on the discrepancy and the shocklike reactions that follow when the aspirant professional perceives that many professional ideals and values are not operational and go unrewarded in the work setting (Kramer, 1974, pp. vii–viii).

The symptoms of reality shock are fear, anger, hate, self-pity, outrage, and withdrawal (Kramer, 1974).

Reality shock — the discovery of a conflict between values learned in school and values operative in the work setting — may be one source of stress that can lead to burnout, but it is not the only such stressor. Cherniss (1980a), for example, mentions reality shock as a source of burnout, but he places it within a more comprehensive model. Similarly, Maslach and Jackson (1978) note that the legal services attorneys they studied were not prepared in law school for interpersonal work with clients, but they note that other stressors are also operative, such as the sheer number of indigent clients who need assistance. Thus, reality shock may be one source of stress that can lead to burnout, but burnout can also be caused by other pressures such as excessive client contact.

Comparison of Burnout and Alienation

A report by the Berkeley Planning Associates used burnout and alienation synonymously and defined burnout as "the extent to which a worker has become separated or withdrawn from the original meaning or purpose of his work — the degree to which a worker expresses estrangement from clients, coworkers and agency" (cited in Cherniss, 1980b, p. 16). A more traditional definition of alienation, however, is the description of the problem as the "intrinsic meaninglessness of social roles to the individuals who enact them. If all that ties individuals to organizations are extrinsic factors of reward and punishment, then people may well be alienated both from their work and from society" (Katz & Kahn, 1978, p. 381). Symptoms of alienation are a sense of powerlessness, a sense of meaninglessness, a sense of normlessness, social isolation, value isolation, and self-estrangement (Katz & Kahn, 1978). Concretely, the alienated police officer has been described as "inactive and corruptible. He may view himself as 'doing time,' and going through motions. Conversely, he may see himself engaged in a 'thankless crusade, unappreciated by others" (Toch, 1979, p. 7).

Certainly, there are some similarities between alienation and burnout. The Berkeley Planning Associates' definition of alienation-burnout is very similar to Maslach's description of depersonalization as one aspect of burnout and perhaps to her description of extreme lack of personal accomplishment. There is also similarity to Edelwich's description of apathy as the fourth stage of the burnout process. Likewise Toch's (1979)

depiction of the alienated police officer sounds very similar to a description of burned out cops (Maslach & Jackson, 1979).

As was the case with reality shock, however, alienation does not include all the aspects of the burnout process. In other words, burnout does refer to a sense of detachment from one's job, especially from clients, but it also includes chronic fatigue and cynicism (Maslach, 1982). Also, alienation carries overtones of ideological discontent whereas burnout does not. For example, Karger has advocated redefining burnout as alienation in order to change the perspective from that of the subjective and the interpersonal to the objective and the bureaucratic where alienation (burnout) can be seen in its true light as

> a functional response to the dehumanizing, mechanistic, and overwhelming chore of participating in a program geared for financial rather than public accountability. . . . Public welfare is, in itself, a microcosm of the social reality — a subordination of human interaction to the reified world of production. The public welfare worker is strained by the demands of his or her profession, the agency, clients, and the community. It may be the contradiction inherent in these demands that contributes to burnout (Karger, 1981, p. 280).

Comparison of Burnout and Job Satisfaction

It is important to distinguish burnout from job (dis)satisfaction for several reasons. First, at least some writers confuse the two concepts. For example, Harrison (1980) has equated the two terms and used a measure of job satisfaction, the Job Descriptive Index, to measure burnout. Second, two of the pioneering researchers on burnout, Maslach and Jackson (1981), have been careful to distinguish the two concepts. Third, much of the previous research on job-related problems has centered on job satisfaction. Ten years ago Locke (1976), for example, noted 3,300 studies of job satisfaction. Fourth, some of the research on probation officers has used the concept of job satisfaction as its conceptual framework (Polisky, 1981a, 1981b).

Defining job satisfaction is fraught with more difficulties than is defining burnout (see, e.g., Cope, 1979). Some writers define job satisfaction very broadly: "Positive attitudes toward the job are conceptually equivalent to job satisfaction and negative attitudes toward the job are equivalent to job dissatisfaction" (Vroom, 1964, p. 99). Similarly, Locke defines satisfaction "as a pleasurable or positive emotional state resulting from the appraisal of one's job or job experiences" (Locke, 1976, p. 1300). Others stress the importance of distinguishing between general job satisfaction ("overall liking for the job situation") and intrinsic job satisfaction, which is satisfaction "deriving from the content of the work process" (Katz & Kahn, 1978, pp. 364–66). As noted below, there is also extrinsic satisfaction. Finally, Herzberg (1976) has contended that satisfaction and dissatisfaction are not opposite ends of the same continuum but represent two distinct continua or phenomena. That is, satisfaction refers to the extent that a job contributes to a worker's growth needs while dissatisfaction refers to the extent that a job does not promote the avoidance of pain (Herzberg, 1976).

In light of this discussion of job satisfaction what is the difference between job satisfaction and burnout? If one defines burnout as "negative feelings about the work itself" (Harrison, 1980, p. 42), then burnout is identical to a definition of job dissatisfaction as "negative attitudes toward the job" (Vroom, 1964, p. 99), and it makes sense to measure burnout with a traditional measure of job satisfaction. However, the more fruitful approach seems to be that job satisfaction itself can refer to overall or global satisfaction, intrinsic satisfaction, and extrinsic satisfaction. Overall job satisfaction is a very general appraisal of one's job. Intrinsic satisfaction refers to an appraisal of one's job in terms of the work itself, such as how much challenge the job offers. Extrinsic satisfaction refers to an appraisal of factors that are separate from the nature of the work one does, such as the important questions of office lighting, ventilation, and pay. Because burnout refers to a process of coping or adapting to chronic stress, it seems clearest to say that job dissatisfaction, in any of its three aspects, can be a source of stress that may lead to burnout. This is the approach of Cherniss (1980b) and seems to be congruent with Maslach and Jackson's (1981) insistence that burnout and job satisfaction are distinct concepts of distinct phenomena.

What adds some confusion to the picture is that Maslach has called one aspect of burnout lack of personal accomplishment and one subscale of her burnout inventory measures this dimension of "feelings of [lack of] competence and successful achievement in one's work" (Maslach & Jackson, 1981, p. 3). Although Maslach and Jackson found that this scale correlated only weakly with a measure of overall job satisfaction, it is possible that this scale may simply measure intrinsic job satisfaction. More about this issue will be discussed later (see Chapter 5). Here it is important simply to note that one very important measure of job burnout may include a measure of intrinsic job satisfaction.

Comparison of Burnout and Job Stress

Stress and job stress have become household words in U.S. society. Today people still read and cite the pioneering work of Hans Selye (1976) on stress in general and the seminal work on job stress conducted at the University of Michigan (Kahn, Wolfe, Quinn, Snoek, & Rosenthal, 1964). This concern with stress in general and job stress in particular has received a great deal of attention in the field of criminal justice. Although research on the job stress experienced by police officers was the first focus of criminal justice researchers (e.g., Kroes, Margolis, & Hurrell, 1974; see Malloy & Mays, 1984, for a recent review), recent years have seen a number of studies on the job stress of correctional officers (Cheek & Miller, 1983; Cullen, Link, Wolfe, & Frank, 1985; Lindquist & Whitehead, 1986a; Philiber, 1987). There has even been a study of stress among correctional teachers (Belcastro, Gold, & Grant, 1982).

Because stress is so critical to many definitions of burnout (Cherniss 1980a, 1980b; Maslach, 1982), it is necessary to examine the concepts of stress and job stress to better understand burnout.

In his writing on stress, Selye defined stress as "the nonspecific response of the body to any demand" (Selye, 1976, p. 1). Selye used "stress" as the response to a demand or "stressor"; others use the word "stress" as a stressor, that is, as a factor leading to the response that they label "strain" (e.g., Katz & Kahn, 1978).

More recent analyses of stress (see, e.g., Caplan, 1985, Pearlin, Lieberman, Menaghan, & Mullan, 1981) see Selye's emphasis on demands leading to stress as important but too narrow and therefore have defined stress more broadly:

> Stress is now widely viewed, not merely as something exogenous, but as the product of a dynamic mismatch between the individual and his/her physical or social environment. This interactive view of stress holds that situations are not inherently stressful; rather it is the combination of the particular situation and an individual, with his specific personality, behavioral pattern, and life-situation circumstances, that results in a stress producing imbalance (McMichael, 1978, p. 128).

This view has been called the person-environment fit perspective on stress (Kasl, 1980) or the interactive perspective (Chesney & Roseman, 1980). It is broader than the narrower demand perspective of Selye in that it sees any mismatch between the person and the environment as possibly stressful. Thus, too many demands may represent a mismatch for one worker, while too few demands may be stressful for another worker who has the skill and the desire to be very active.

Concerning the relationship of stress to burnout, it seems most helpful to repeat Cherniss's (1980b) observation that job stress and burnout are not synonymous but that intense and chronic stress can lead to burnout, especially if the worker is helpless to change the situation. More fully, burnout is an intrapsychic defense against stress when the stress problem cannot be solved in an active way or when the worker chooses an intrapsychic method of coping — "one which emphasizes withdrawal, detachment, avoidance, lowering of goals, and blaming others" (Cherniss, 1980b, p. 47) — rather than direct action.

CONCLUSION

Several definitions of burnout have been reviewed. Although there are some variations, it seems that most of the writers on job burnout have been describing the same phenomenon: a process of coping with intense, chronic stress on the job. Burnout is related to other concepts that have been used to describe job-related problems, such as reality shock, alienation, job satisfaction, and job stress, but burnout is distinguishable from these concepts.

In the following chapters, two definitions of burnout, those of Maslach and her colleagues and Cherniss, will be emphasized. Maslach's definition is important because of her pioneering research on the problem and because of the widespread acceptance of her measure of burnout. Cherniss's definition is important because of his research on the topic and because he has provided a comprehensive model of the burnout process.

Chapter 3 examines causal models of the burnout process, with particular attention to the efforts of Maslach and Cherniss.

The Causes of Burnout 3

Chapter 2 showed that burnout can be conceptualized as a psychic defense to the chronic and intense stress of work in human service jobs. To clarify this definition, it is necessary to examine the causes or sources of job burnout and to attempt to construct a causal model of the burnout process.

To achieve this goal, this chapter will review the literature on the sources of burnout, especially the more complete attempts to present a causal model. The chapter will conclude with an evaluative summary of previous research on the sources of burnout that serves as a guide for much of the research in this book.

THREE PRELIMINARY MODELS OF THE BURNOUT PROCESS

Harrison (1980), Pines and Kafry (1978), and Edelwich (1980) have offered rudimentary models of the burnout process. These models will be discussed before moving on to more complex models of the burnout process.

Harrison's Model

As noted in Chapter 2, Harrison (1980) equates burnout with job dissatisfaction or "negative feelings about the work itself" (Harrison, 1980, p. 42). He goes on to argue that these negative feelings "occur in large part because the work does not encourage or allow for the worker's psychological growth, a feature on which many social workers undoubtedly place a high value" (Harrison, 1980, p. 42). As he borrows the Job Descriptive Index to measure job dissatisfaction-burnout, so also Harrison borrows the role theory of Kahn and his colleagues (1964) to postulate that role conflict and role ambiguity are the critical causal variables leading to burnout: "Role conflict results when incompatible or tenuously compatible demands or expectations are placed upon the social worker. Role ambiguity is a lack of clarity as to what is expected, appropriate, or effective behavior. Both appear as common problem areas in the protective-services specialization" (Harrison, 1980, p. 32).

In a test of this model on 112 social workers in Minnesota, Harrison found support for role ambiguity as a source of burnout but not for role conflict; therefore, he has revised his model to focus only on the impact of lack of role clarity as a cause of burnout. He is optimistic about intervention efforts because he feels that role ambiguity is "at least partially amenable to change efforts" (Harrison, 1980, p. 43).

Pines and Kafry's Model of Tedium

In their research on occupational tedium, as they prefer to label the problem, Pines and Kafry note two sources of burnout. First, although most human relations are symmetrical in that they involve give and take on both sides, social work or therapeutic relations are complementary: "One person gives and the other receives" (Pines & Kafry, 1978, p. 499). Second, social work necessarily involves direct emotional confrontations, which often result in emotional reactions on the part of the worker; it is hard to remain aloof when a client is distraught.

Pines and Kafry go on to suggest that both internal and external characteristics of social work can lead to stress and tedium. By internal characteristics, Pines and Kafry mean that the absence of variety, autonomy, significance (accomplishment), success in performance, and feedback can be problematic; persons who report lower levels of one or more of these characteristics should report higher tedium scores. External characteristics of the job refer to "properties of the work environment" (Pines & Kafry, 1978, p. 501) such as the quality of work relations with colleagues, superiors, and subordinates, the sharing of responsibilities (e.g., team approaches), support, time-out opportunities (chances to withdraw temporarily from the work environment), and social feedback on one's performance. The more positive a worker's scores on these external characteristics, the less tedium should be present. Finally, these external characteristics are hypothesized to be more critical than the internal characteristics.

A third general source of stress and, eventually, tedium in social work is a set of organizational variables emphasizing "the quality requirements that are built into an organization's specific definition of a job" (Pines & Kafry, 1978, p. 502). This set includes pay satisfaction, caseload size, job level (line worker versus supervisor), and work schedule.

A test of the model on 120 social workers revealed that all of the external characteristics were correlated significantly with occupational tedium but that feedback was the only internal characteristic significantly related to tedium. All of the organizational variables except pay satisfaction were significantly related to tedium. Pines and Kafry conclude that the importance of the external factors suggests "that social workers may be more than normally sensitive to people as sources of both emotional stress and support" and that the importance of the organizational variables shows the importance of "the quality requirements built into the employing organization's structure" (Pines & Kafry, 1978, p. 506).

Edelwich's Model of the Burnout Process

As noted in Chapter 2, Edelwich (1980) proposes a four-stage burnout process: enthusiasm, stagnation, frustration, and apathy. Progression through these stages is neither linear nor inevitable, but cyclic. Thus, the process can begin again, and intervention can be effective if it is timely.

Each stage has its respective source or sources of burnout. Stage one, idealistic enthusiasm, often lasts for the first six months of one's first human service job. Its source lies in the discrepancy between the beginning worker's expectations and reality, such as unrealistic expectations about effecting decisive changes in clients and expectations of dramatic gains in status and recognition for the worker. In the second stage, stagnation, the worker begins to see that he will not always or often be rewarded by superiors or appreciated by clients. One sees that results are elusive and that one's enthusiastic idealism has led to overinvestment in the job to the exclusion of other interests. At this point the concrete frustration of the job such as low motivation in clients can lead to a sobering of attitudes that can be intensified by the contagion of other workers' pessimistic attitudes. Also, stagnation can arise from the low pay of many social service jobs and the realization that the work may be dead-end in terms of career possibilities, especially for persons without a graduate degree. In stage three, frustration, the limitations of the job go beyond affecting the worker's satisfaction to "threatening to defeat the purpose of what one is doing" (Edelwich, 1980, p. 29). At this stage, the sources of frustration such as low pay, excessive hours and paperwork, lack of appreciation by clients and supervisors, working in a system that is not responsive to client needs, and so on are not different from problems at stages one and two, but the effect is more pervasive. The final stage of the burnout process is apathy: "a progressive emotional detachment in the face of frustration" (Edelwich, 1980, p. 164).

Apathy can lead to leaving the field or to remaining on the job to support oneself but giving up the fight: "putting in the minimum required time . . . , avoiding challenges (even avoiding clients whenever possible), and seeking mainly to keep from endangering the secure position that compensates, however inadequately, for the loss of job satisfaction" (Edelwich, 1980, p. 29). This stage of apathy takes the longest to reach and is the most difficult in which to intervene.

Comments on the Models

Some comments are in order on these three models of Harrison, Pines and Kafry, and Edelwich. First, the research evidence on all three is limited. Harrison and Pines and Kafry tested their models on small samples of only about 100 workers each; Edelwich derived his model from observation and workshops he conducted. Second, Harrison's model is extremely limited in that he examined only two independent variables: role ambiguity and role conflict. Although the models of Pines and Kafry and Edelwich are more complex, neither has specified a concise set of propositions. Both are basically multifactor models stipulating a potpourri of independent variables, although Edelwich does propose a sequencing of the burnout process, a key ingredient to any explanation of a dynamic process.

CHERNISS'S MODELS OF THE BURNOUT PROCESS

Cary Cherniss has offered two models of the burnout process: a limited model and a comprehensive one. Both deserve attention.

The Limited Model

The limited model is based on Cherniss's (1980a) personological or in-depth interviews with 28 new public professionals: lawyers, high school teachers, mental health workers, and public health nurses employed in public agencies rather than in private practice. Cherniss focused on public professionals because more and more professionals are working in public, bureaucratic settings.

The model is simple: stressors lead to stress for the worker who then chooses to cope or is constrained to cope by negative changes in attitude rather than by active problem solving. For example, workers become cynical or blame clients for their problems rather than engage in efforts to solve client problems or problems in the work setting.

To fill in this sketch, Cherniss (1980a) notes that several sources of stress (stressors) are possible in the public professions. One such stressor is doubting one's competence because of inadequate training or training that resulted in the impression that one was prepared for immediate success without a period of experiential learning on the job. Related stressors are a new worker's disappointment at finding less excitement and meaning in professional work than was expected and the unexpected finding that colleagues are often too busy to be collegial. Other stressors are disappointment with clients who lack the motivation or ability or both to change and bureaucratic infringement on the worker's autonomy in trying to meet client needs.

If the worker cannot solve these problems, there are several possible strategies to cope with the stress. One is to scale down one's initial goals and aspirations — to settle for less. A related coping mechanism is to decrease one's sense of responsibility for the results of one's work; the workers "increasingly blamed the clients or the system when efforts to help fell short" (Cherniss, 1980a, p. 209). A third possibility is to become more cynical, pessimistic, and conservative about clients and people in general; clients are seen in a less positive light and "bad guys" such as police officers are seen in a more positive light. Increasing emotional detachment is the fourth possible attitude change, and the fifth is an increasing psychological withdrawal from work and a greater investment in nonwork pursuits as a "source of fulfillment, meaning, and stimulation in life" (Cherniss, 1980a, p. 210).

Cherniss notes that several factors in the work setting were associated with differences in the degree of burnout found in the workers he interviewed. One such factor was the presence of an orientation program sensitive to the problems of beginning workers. Work load size was also important because it allowed more time for clients and thus a greater chance of success. Third, the four types of jobs studied varied in the amount of stimulation provided. Scope of client contact was also important; greater scope allowed workers to see more aspects of their clients' lives and thereby react more positively to them. Greater autonomy reduced stress as did higher congruence between institutional goals and professional service goals. Concerning leadership, these new professionals preferred supervisors who offered support without unduly infringing on autonomy. Availability of coworkers for support also influenced variations in workers' experiences of burnout; for example, the high school teachers felt isolated in their classrooms.

The personal factor of career orientation — "the meaning of work for the individual" (Cherniss, 1980a, p. 189) — was also an important factor in the burnout process. Social activists, idealists seeking to bring about social and institutional change, and artisans, those interested more in the intrinsic quality of their work than in financial success or advancement, were more likely to experience frustration. Less likely to experience disappointment were careerists, those seeking success, prestige, and respectability, and self-investors, those more interested in their personal lives outside work. In addition to career orientation, the quality of one's personal life was an important determinant of stress at work; stress at home or lack of support from friends and/or family could add to any stress experienced in the workplace (Cherniss, 1980a, p. 211).

The Comprehensive Model

In a second book, which is based on his own research and reviews of the job stress and burnout literature, Cherniss (1980b) has presented a more complete model of the burnout process. Here burnout is defined as a defensive coping reaction to intense and chronic stress; stress is defined as the short-term emotional response to an imbalance between demands and resources (Cherniss, 1980b, pp. 17–18). The model of the burnout process includes discussion of the dynamics of job stress, the organizational design as a source of burnout, the effect of support, the relation of individual factors to burnout, and an examination of the historical and cultural sources of burnout.

Concerning the dynamics of job stress, Cherniss (1980b) reiterates that stress involves a situation in which demands do not match resources. This can refer to either an excess of demands over resources or a lack of demands, a lack of stimulation, for the resourceful worker. Furthermore, demands can be external and/or internal; they can be stipulated by a supervisor and/or by one's own desires or sense of values. Second, burnout involves a choice of intrapsychic coping rather than active problem solving, a choice much more frequent in "situations characterized by high ambiguity, conflict, and helplessness" (Cherniss, 1980b, p. 48). Third, earlier research has indicated that one critical demand of human service workers is achieving a sense of efficacy: "the demand for competent, effective performance" (Cherniss, 1980b, pp. 48–49). Human service workers want to have an impact on the people with whom they work, to the extent that the work is seen as a calling and not just a job. Unfortunately they face compounding factors such as lack of feedback, the problem of authorship (being able to claim responsibility when clients do change), and client resistance to change.

A key element in Cherniss's model of burnout is the organizational design: "the formal, rational properties of an organization that can be readily controlled by those responsible for designing and/or managing a program" (Cherniss, 1980b, p. 79). Organizational design includes the role structure, the power structure, and the normative structure of a human service organization.

Role structure refers to how tasks and duties are allocated. Unfortunately, a program's role structure often promotes role conflict and role ambiguity, which in turn lead to job stress (see, e.g., Kahn, Wolfe, Quinn, Snoek, & Rosenthal, 1964).

Role conflict can take several forms. The most obvious is role overload where demands exceed the worker's resources of time and effort. High caseloads, for example, dictate inadequate care for many clients and also prevent workers from having the time to seek solutions to client problems. Cherniss does not seem to distinguish between quantitative overload (having too much work to do) and qualitative overload (having work that is too difficult to do or to do well given the constraints in the situation), a distinction that others emphasize (Katz & Kahn, 1978). A second type of role conflict is intersender conflict where a worker is receiving opposing messages from different role senders. A juvenile probation officer, for example, may be receiving one message to be a counselor and another to be an agent of social control (Cherniss, 1980b). A third type of role conflict is person-role conflict, the internal conflict where "the role requires certain behavior that is inconsistent with the role player's motives, abilities, or moral values" (Cherniss, 1980b, p. 83). One example of this type of conflict in human service work is the conflict that occurs when the worker desires or has been trained to be a specialist but the organization expects the worker to be a generalist. A more specific example is the conflict for workers who want to operate according to a professional service ideal that emphasizes the needs of the client but face the bureaucratic constraints of "orderliness, standardization, uniformity, efficiency, public accountability, and impersonality" (Cherniss, 1980b, p. 86). This professional-bureaucratic role conflict is especially vexing because new professionals expect autonomy rather than bureaucratic interference.

Following Kahn, Wolfe, Quinn, Snoek, and Rosenthal (1964), Cherniss (1980b, p. 89) defines role ambiguity as a lack of "the information necessary for adequate performance of the role." One example would be a directive to concentrate on the "important aspects" of the job without any clarification of what those "important aspects" are. Another problem is the presence of ambiguous goals as opposed to clear, concrete objectives in the agency. Finally, Cherniss notes that role ambiguity, measured by the perceived amount and clarity of communication, was the second most important predictor of burnout in one study (Cherniss, 1980b, p. 91).

The role structure of a program can also contribute to burnout in its impact on the motivating potential of the job, that is, "the extent to which the job is stimulating and meaningful" (Cherniss, 1980b, p. 92). One important factor in the motivating potential of the job is variety, both the number of different tasks a worker is allocated as well as the number of client groups one works with. For example, one who only counsels and counsels only drug addicts is more likely to be bored and burn out than a worker who also does consulting and sees nonaddicts as well as addicts. A second aspect of the motivating potential of the job is task identity, which means that too much specialization and fragmentation can lead to the feeling that the worker is unable to see how his/her efforts contribute to the overall intervention effort (Cherniss, 1980b, p. 93). The presence of opportunities for learning is a third job design factor that contributes to meaning and stimulation. Such opportunities can reduce the feeling that the worker is only giving and not receiving and thereby reduce boredom. Two additional factors are the availability of feedback on client progress and information from supervisors about one's own progress and about the agency in general. Feedback and information "contribute to stimulation at the same time that they reduce ambiguity and the potential for failure" (Cherniss, 1980b, p. 96). One problem here is that the feedback frequently found in human services, selectively negative feedback (news about one's failures), is not helpful.

A second major aspect of organizational design that influences burnout is the power structure: how decisions are made. Reviewing a considerable amount of research, Cherniss concludes that greater autonomy and participation in decision making enable staff to experience greater control, which in turn serves to prevent a feeling of helplessness that leads to the defensive coping of burnout. The hierarchical power structure found in public agencies, however,

> frustrates the staff person's quest for psychological success. Even when organizational imperatives are consistent with client welfare, the staff person increasingly feels like a small, easily replaceable cog in a large wheel. Burnout is an all-too-common consequence when autonomy and control are limited by the power structure of a human service (Cherniss, 1980b, p. 102).

The third major component of organizational design is the normative structure of a program: its goals, norms, and ideology (Cherniss, 1980b, p. 102). A treatment philosophy that is concrete, accepted, and used is helpful in reducing burnout insofar as it aids in fostering goal clarity and reducing role ambiguity. The strength of the bureaucratic mentality is a second aspect of the normative structure related to burnout. The more an organization encourages innovation, creativity, and risk taking, the less likely burnout is to occur. Third, an emphasis on research as an organizational goal can reduce burnout by providing increased opportunities for stimulation and success. Fourth, if the organization has norms that value the staff and their concerns, then burnout is less likely to occur. If the organization, however, neglects or opposes staff concerns, the "staff are likely to feel that they are powerless to change working conditions that contribute to stress. Change seems futile. A sense of helplessness increasingly pervades such settings, and the burnout rate is high" (Cherniss, 1980b, p. 108).

Additional factors in preventing burnout are the leadership in the organization and the quality of staff interaction and support. The ideal supervisor combines the right level of support with sufficient allowance for the individual worker's need for autonomy; poor supervisors are "frequently unavailable and/or dictatorial and arbitrary" (Cherniss, 1980b, p. 116). Also, supervisors can prevent burnout by acting as advocates or buffers for front-line workers against the community or against higher-level authorities; that is, supervisors can be of assistance by giving the impression that they are championing the interests of the workers outside the agency. Like supervisors, fellow staff members can be supportive by offering advice and information or by allowing for cathartic experiences in which tension can be released and perspective gained. Furthermore, colleagues can provide a framework or reference point for one to measure the quality of one's work, can buffer pressures from the community or upper management, and can be a source of stimulation in discussions of work experiences. Sometimes staff interaction exacerbates job stress. An example of this is a meeting that degenerates into a gripe session instead of being cathartic, informational, or stimulating. Also, clashes over differing theoretical orientations or competition over scarce resources or status can prevent positive interaction among staff members.

Personality factors can also affect one's vulnerability to burnout. First, human service work seems to attract individuals who possess traits associated with neurotic anxiety:

> [U]nfortunately, the human services may attract individuals who have strong dependency and achievement needs, set unrealistically high standards for themselves, and display other traits associated with neurotic anxiety. They are people who want to "rescue" others and who feel miserable when they fail (Cherniss, 1980b, p. 129).

Also attracted to human service work and also susceptible to burnout are the Type A personalities who are competitive and feel pressured by time constraints (Cherniss, 1980b, p. 130). Similarly, previous research has led Cherniss to conclude that persons with an external locus of control (who feel that they are not in control of their own destinies) and introverts (who tend to withdraw from others who could be sources of support) are more likely to experience burnout. Despite the possible importance of personality, however, Cherniss concludes that personality factors should not be overestimated because "[T]he structure of the job and work organization ultimately is a stronger determinant of the incidence of burnout than is the individual's personality makeup" (Cherniss, 1980b, p. 131).

Another factor more important than personality is career orientation: the goals, values, and attitudes one seeks in a job. One typology of career orientation distinguishes the professional orientation from the bureaucratic orientation: The professional orientation emphasizes the uniqueness of both the client and the professional. Autonomy and collegial authority are emphasized. The bureaucratic orientation emphasizes efficiency, standardization, and subservience to a central organizational authority (Cherniss, 1980b, p. 132). Research suggests that individuals who rate high on both dimensions seem the most susceptible to burnout, followed by those who are high on professional values and low on bureaucratic values (Cherniss, 1980b, p. 133). A second way to classify career orientations is to distinguish among artisans, careerists, self-investors, and social activists, as noted earlier in the discussion of Cherniss's (1980a) more basic model.

Past experience can affect one's current reactions to stress and thereby to burnout. In general, previous mastery of stressful situations reduces current susceptibility to stress and makes one ready to accept new challenges. An interesting exception to this general rule, however, is that workers with postgraduate training, workers who have ostensibly mastered the stress of such training, have been found to be more susceptible to stress than less educated workers (Cherniss, 1980b, p. 137).

A final personal factor that may influence one's reaction to stress is the quality of one's life after or outside of work. If they do not impose demands that conflict with job demands, friends and relatives can be important sources of support. Interestingly, there has been evidence that married individuals are less likely to experience burnout than single or divorced persons but that children can make a worker less able to accommodate to job stress than can a worker without children (Cherniss, 1980b, pp. 138–40). Finally, outside activities can offer an alternative source of gratification, or they can introduce a worker to new friends who can become new sources of social support (Cherniss, 1980b, pp. 138–39).

Cherniss concludes his model with comments on the historical and cultural sources of burnout, such as an alleged decline in the sense of community and a legacy from the 1960s and 1970s that poverty, racism, and related problems are overwhelming conundrums impervious to intervention (Cherniss, 1980b, pp. 114–50). Of more immediate concern to human service professionals is Cherniss's observation that we live in an age of psychology with unrealistic expectations for meaning, novelty, and fulfillment in work. Furthermore, on the one hand, there is the professional mystique that implies that educational credentials alone prepare one for immediate success, that professionals always have high degrees of autonomy and control in the work setting, that clients are both cooperative and grateful, that the work is meaningful and stimulating, and that coworkers are collegial. Reality, on the other hand, entails deficient training, bureaucratic work settings, indifferent clients, routine tasks, and unsympathetic colleagues (Cherniss, 1980b, p. 154). In short, the professional mystique involves a set of unrealistic expectations that make the new professional ripe for burnout.

Cherniss himself has not offered a multivariate test of his model, but an independent test of many of the key concepts of the model did offer "considerable empirical support" (Burke, Shearer, & Deszca, 1984, p. 183). Specifically, a study of more than 400 police officers showed that work setting and stress antecedents were correlated with burnout but that "individual career orientations produced only weak correlations with burnout" (Burke, Shearer, & Deszca, 1984, p. 183, 186).

MASLACH'S BURNOUT MODEL

As noted in Chapter 2, Maslach — and her most frequent collaborator, Jackson — defines burnout as the result of an inability to cope successfully with job stress that then manifests itself in one or more of three aspects: emotional exhaustion, depersonalization, and lack of personal accomplishment (Maslach, 1982; Maslach & Jackson, 1981). Emotional exhaustion implies an inability to give of oneself at the psychological level. Depersonalization refers to negative, cynical, and detached feelings about clients to the point that workers objectify clients (treat them as things rather than full human subjects) or even ridicule or blame clients for their troubles. Lack of personal accomplishment means that "workers feel unhappy about themselves and dissatisfied with their accomplishments on the job" (Maslach & Jackson, 1981, p. 99). At one time Maslach and Jackson (1980) implied that these three phenomena of emotional exhaustion, depersonalization, and lack of personal accomplishment were sequential phases, but her present terminology is that they are three "aspects" of the one phenomenon of burnout (Maslach & Jackson, 1981; Jackson, Schwab, & Schuler, 1986) without any implication of a sequence.

Concerning etiology, Maslach is convinced that burnout is not caused by individual or personality factors but that it is

> best understood (and modified) in terms of situational sources of job-related, interpersonal stress. The phenomenon is so widespread, the people affected by it are so numerous, and their personalities and backgrounds so varied, that it does not make sense to identify "bad people" as the cause for what is clearly an undesirable outcome. Rather, we should be trying to identify and analyze the critical components of "bad" situations in which many good people function (Maslach, 1982, pp. 9–10).

An important source of burnout is client contact; the crucial problem is actual, close, continuous contact with clients because it involves cognitive, sensory, and emotional overload (Pines & Maslach, 1980, p. 6). Clients come to the worker with problems and they often come in angry, frightened, and emotionally overwhelmed:

> Helpers are also on the receiving end of some very strong emotions of anger, fear, and frustration. Although they are not the direct cause of the person's plight, they may symbolize those causes or at least the forces that are preventing the person from achieving a solution to his or her problem (Maslach, 1982, p. 20).

Furthermore, the focus on problems in human service work means that the worker focuses on the weaknesses of the client and does not really see the person's strengths and assets and does not see the client once the problem is solved. Also, many client problems show little possibility for improvement or may lead the worker to overidentify with either the problem or the client (Maslach, 1982).

Maslach notes that lack of challenge can cause burnout. This can occur when client problems are similar and repetitive, as may occur among lawyers doing legal service work (Maslach & Jackson, 1978). Also if the worker is seeking self-fulfillment rather than client progress, burnout can result. Excessively idealistic goals are also unrealistic and can lead to burnout (Maslach, 1976; Maslach & Jackson, 1978).

Maslach argues that support at work is an important moderator of burnout because opportunities to discuss problems allow fellow workers to offer support, advice, and the awareness that one is not unique in experiencing problems (Maslach, 1976). Such support can be either formal or informal but, negatively, can degenerate into "bitch" sessions (Maslach, 1978).

Besides support, there are some other ways to deal with burnout such as opportunities for temporary withdrawals from client contact (time-outs) and opportunities for varied work duties. Both of these approaches at least temporarily remove the stress of client contact (Maslach, 1976). Furthermore, because they are sanctioned and provision is made for meeting the needs of clients while the worker is doing something else, the worker need not feel the guilt that is associated with unauthorized work breaks. Outside the workplace, things such as exercise, a daily return to one's private life — especially if that private life involves friends and loved ones, and vacations can attenuate the stress that can lead to burnout.

One must not overemphasize the personal solutions to burnout and neglect the need for organizational change:

> First, although individual coping techniques may be quicker and easier, improvements of the work place may have a more pervasive and long-lasting impact on rates of burnout. Teaching people how to cope with a stressful job is certainly helpful, but it may not be as effective as making the job less stressful to begin with. Second, organizational changes acknowledge the significance of the situation in burnout. This can counter the overwhelming (and somewhat erroneous) tendency to blame either oneself or one's recipients. Third, an organizational response to burnout constitutes recognition of it as a legitimate problem. . . . Once organizations recognize that burnout is a real and serious problem for them and their employees, then greater efforts may be made to deal effectively with it (Maslach, 1982, pp. 118–19).

Like Cherniss, Maslach has not conducted a thorough test of her model. She and Jackson (1984a), however, have suggested that feedback, control (i.e., participation in decision making), and role clarity are critical sources of burnout.

Maslach's associate, Jackson, along with Schuler and Schwab (1986) recently tested these assumptions about the sources of burnout on approximately 250 teachers. Based on the notion that burnout is not a unitary but a complex concept (Maslach & Jackson, 1984a; see also Chapter 2), Jackson and her colleagues hypothesized different antecedents and consequences for each of the three distinct aspects of burnout and found the following:

> Unmet expectations about the job appear not to be associated with burnout. Emotional exhaustion was most strongly associated with role conflict. Feelings of personal accomplishment are highest for teachers in supportive environments, with support from one's principal appearing to be particularly important. Contrary to our predictions, lack of support from one's principal was also the only condition associated with depersonalization (Jackson, Schuler, & Schwab, 1986, pp. 636–37).

Jackson, Schuler, and Schwab went on to observe that the low correlations they found between caseload and burnout may be attributable to the fact that "caseload size is confounded with type of job and type of client contact (telephone versus face to face)" (1986, p. 638). Thus, the measurement of caseload needs to be refined in future research to reflect the complexity of the concept.

Golembiewski, Munzenrider, and Stevenson (1986) also offer some comments on the sources of burnout. Because they rely on the Maslach Burnout Inventory — amended to reflect nine phases — it seems appropriate to note their comments at this juncture.

Golembiewski, Munzenrider, and Stevenson's (1986) research does not support "a substantial locus for burnout in the properties of individuals" (p. 179). Instead, various job and organizational characteristics seem critical: "Involvement, supervisor support, autonomy, clarity and physical comfort are significantly greater in HiBo [High Burnout] than in LoBo [Low Burnout], as expected. In addition, work pressure is significantly less in LoBo than HiBo, which implies few or no cases of laissez-faire supervision in the latter work groups" (p. 190). Because they found strong associations between properties of the immediate work group and burnout, the intact work team is a critical place for intervention, rather than stranger workshops. As Cherniss (1980a, 1980b) has observed, Golembiewski, Munzenrider, and Stevenson find burnout can stem from either overstimulation or understimulation. Finally, there is no simple, one-shot solution to burnout; in fact, "an intervention useful at some phases of burnout may be pointless at other phases, or even poison" (p. 216).

Maslach and her colleagues suggest that client contact, with its inherent possibility of emotional outpouring and reaction, is stressful and can lead to burnout. Other factors such as unrealistic goals, lack of training, and organizations with little support for line workers are mentioned, but the dominant theme is one of emotional overload that is coped with in negative or defensive ways such as withdrawal or distancing oneself from the client.

COMMENTS ON THE CHERNISS AND MASLACH MODELS

Several comments are in order after this tracing of the Cherniss and Maslach models of burnout. First, to call either writer's comments on burnout a "model" is somewhat of a reification. Both have written extensively on burnout, but neither has set forth specific propositions comprising a clear burnout theory. Neither has tested his or her implied propositions, although others have begun this process (Burke, Shearer, & Deszca, 1984; Jackson, Schuler, & Schwab, 1986).

Second, the Cherniss and Maslach starting points seem basically similar: stressors lead to stress, which, if intense and persistent, leads to burnout. Similarly, the two models share many of the same variables as sources of burnout, such as overload and role conflict.

Third, Cherniss's comprehensive model appears to subsume his first model and Maslach's model. That is, his second model seems to be so comprehensive that it includes his first model and Maslach's model and the other models outlined in this chapter. Although other models may stress one or a few aspects of burnout, such as the Maslach emphasis on the stress of client contact as the central source of burnout, Cherniss allows room for those factors and also includes other factors such as the problem of understimulation. In short, Cherniss's model seems to be the most useful model of burnout because it offers the most comprehensive analysis. Although Maslach (1982) and her colleague Jackson (Maslach & Jackson, 1984a; Jackson, Schuler, & Schwab, 1986) have expanded their conceptualization of the burnout process toward a more comprehensive view that approaches the scope of Cherniss's model, Cherniss's model still seems to be the benchmark for future research. Available research on the models seems to offer more support for the Cherniss model (Burke, Shearer, & Deszca, 1984) than for the Maslach-Jackson model (Jackson, Schuler, & Schwab. 1986).

SUMMARY

This chapter has outlined several models of the burnout process, including the models of Cherniss and Maslach. Cherniss's second model appears to be the most comprehensive, including most, if not all, of the variables mentioned in the other models.

In later chapters, data testing some of the key propositions of the Cherniss and Maslach models of the job burnout process is presented, first for probation officers (Chapter 6) and then for correctional officers (Chapter 10). Before that can be done, however, it is necessary to examine the work environment of probation and parole officers to suggest possible sources of burnout in the occupation (Chapter 4). Then it is necessary to explain the study methodology (Chapter 5).

The Conditions of Probation and Parole Employment 4

It appears that burnout is a coping reaction to chronic and intense stress and that various aspects of a job or of an organization can lead to the stress that can cause burnout. Using the framework of Cherniss's (1980b) model (see Chapter 3) of the sources of burnout, this chapter describes some of the job and organizational conditions of probation/parole employment that can lead to stress and burnout.

Except for earlier, partial accounts of the research reported in this book (Whitehead, 1985, 1986a, 1986b, 1987), the term "burnout" has received relatively little attention in the probation/parole literature (e.g., Brown, 1986, 1987). Nevertheless, the probation/parole literature does contain numerous discussions of job problems that burnout theorists contend may lead to burnout.

One preliminary point is that Cherniss (1980a, 1980b) and others (Freudenberger, 1980; Jackson, Schuler, & Schwab, 1986; Maslach, 1982) assume that human service workers begin their jobs as committed and dedicated individuals. Studt's (1973) observation that parole officers she studied began their careers as naive idealists suggests that the same is true in corrections. McCleary's (1978) study of parole officers, however, was ambivalent on this matter. At one point he indicated that the novice parole officers he studied began their careers with a commitment to counseling parolees but were then socialized into office and agency norms against hard work. Elsewhere, however, McCleary contended that "like the rest of us, parole officers are interested in doing as little work as possible" (McCleary, 1978, p. 43). This conclusion does not appear to be a statement about the effect of bureaucratic constraints on individual initiative but a summary judgment of human nature similar to McGregor's (1980) description of Theory X.

Thus, two parole researchers have offered opposing positions on the issue of whether officers begin their careers as dedicated neophytes or as lazy clock watchers. This basic disagreement is not unimportant because burnout writers assume that at some point workers were dedicated. If that is not the case, then burnout could not occur; one has to be on fire with enthusiasm and dedication before one can burn out!

THE JOB OF THE PROBATION/PAROLE OFFICER

Traditionally, both probation and parole have involved supervision of offenders in the community. Historically, supervision has connoted a philanthropic volunteer who is altruistically concerned about persons who would otherwise be behind bars (see, e.g., Allen, Eskridge, Latessa, & Vito, 1985; Gray, 1986; Keve, 1981). Philosophically, supervision connotes one-to-one casework wherein a trained social worker interacts with a willing client (e.g., Ohlin, Piven, & Pappenfort, 1956). In practice, supervision means contact between the officer and the individuals on his/her caseload in the office, at the client's residence, place of employment, on the street, or in jail (if, for example, the offender is being detained pending a new charge). These contacts can vary in length from a few minutes to an hour or more. They can be counseling sessions where serious personal matters are discussed or perfunctory encounters between members of vastly different social worlds, especially if the two worlds happen to be racially or economically distinct, which is often the case.

By statute, supervision means that the probationer or parolee has consented to abide by a set of conditions. Although they vary among jurisdictions, usually such conditions stipulate that the probationer or parolee report to an officer, abide by all laws, notify or petition the officer about any changes in employment status or place of residence, seek employment or education, and, if appropriate, make restitution to the victim. Often special conditions are added, such as a directive to seek psychiatric therapy (see Allen, Eskridge, Latessa, & Vito, 1985, for a thorough discussion of probation conditions). The job of the officer, then, is to monitor the offender's compliance with these conditions and to assist the offender directly or indirectly in complying with the conditions. Direct assistance entails individual or group counseling of offenders and helping offenders find employment. Indirect assistance involves referring offenders to services available in the community; this is often called brokerage or advocacy. In fact, whereas the ideal officer used to be a "jack-of-all-trades" type of officer (Studt, 1973), more recent writers contend that referral activity is more realistic for contemporary officers (Dell'Apa, Adams, Jorgensen, & Sigurdson, 1976; O'Leary & Clear, 1984). While John Augustus, the father of probation, may have had the time and the talent to find jobs and lodging for his charges, the contemporary officer cannot be everything to everyone. He/she can, however, know where in the community an offender might find help for a particular problem. Thus, Dietrich (1979), for example, argues that the prescribed role for the contemporary officer is that of an efficient case manager who can steer clients to appropriate community services.

Both compliance and assistance actions are recorded in a case file or dossier. Theoretically, the case file serves as an aid in the implementation of a treatment plan or intervention strategy for each offender. That is, the officer can review the file, either alone or with an immediate supervisor, to review the offender's progress. McCleary (1978), however, has argued that case folders are often kept purposefully vague so that if the offender commits a new offense or violates a condition of supervision, the officer can interpret the vague record so as to discredit the offender. In this manner, the officer can defend both his/her actions and the department and pave the way for an unobstructed revocation of probation or parole.

Perhaps a more pervasive problem with probation and parole case records is that they are woefully inadequate. A study of federal probation (General Accounting Office, 1976), for example, found that 60 percent of the records reviewed did not contain written treatment plans outlining officers' objectives for probationers.

Another major task of officers is the preparation of reports. Probation officers prepare presentence investigations, reports which judges use at sentencing, on the legal and social status of offenders. Parole officers conduct preparole reports, investigations of an incarcerated offender's plan for parole.

To prepare these reports, officers interview offenders and review court records, police arrest sheets, school records, military records, and previous probation and parole reports. The officer attempts to verify as much information as possible by such record checks and by contacting individuals such as the offender's employer, spouse, and so forth. The officer then summarizes all the information into the report, which usually includes a recommendation about the sentence the offender will receive or the parole decision of the parole board. Blumberg (1979) and others have made some disparaging remarks, discussed later in the chapter, about the process of preparing such reports.

Another major task of probation officers who work with juvenile offenders is intake. Although this is changing (Rubin, 1985), probation officers in juvenile court have acted traditionally as screening agents. If a youth is accused of a delinquent action, it has been the duty of the probation intake officer to interview the affected parties to determine if the matter should be referred to court or if some precourt adjustment can be made.

Many officers perform all three major functions of probation/parole work: supervision, investigation, and intake. (Parole does not include a function comparable to intake.) Such a generalist approach is especially likely in small counties, whereas specialization in one function is often the norm in larger agencies with larger staffs. Specialization, however, is not always absolute; an officer who specializes in supervision may also conduct a few presentence investigations each month.

Because of variations from agency to agency, it is difficult to describe a typical officer's day other than to say it is some combination of the activities of supervision, investigation, and intake. In day-to-day practice, probation and parole often translate into mundane matters such as talking with offenders, visiting them in their homes, writing reports, conferring with supervisors, checking court records, making court appearances, and making phone calls. Interspersed among these activities are the activities that constitute life in any office: talking with coworkers, sharing gossip, and discussing managerial policies. Such activities take place in the office proper, in the coffee room, at lunch, and outside the office whenever and wherever officers meet. (For a series of probation officer vignettes, see Thomson and Fogel, 1980.)

What this depiction probably omits is the somewhat amorphous character of probation and parole work. The depiction sets out the framework of probation/parole activities, but the precise articulation of that framework into a completed workday or workweek varies with the individual office and the individual officer. Different offices will have different policies. One former probation director, for example, established a policy that none of his officers would carry a gun despite the fact that officers were peace officers by state law and thereby authorized to carry a weapon. This director was also opposed to the formation of any type of warrant squad whereby officers would serve their own warrants on probationers in violation of any supervision condition. In other words, the director sought to establish a social work ethos or climate for the agency compared to a law enforcement climate. Individual officers, however, actually carry out policy, and some officers in this agency carried guns contrary to agency policy. Some officers followed a law enforcement emphasis in other ways, for example, by interrogating probationers instead of counseling them during office visits. Other officers were more liberal than the director. Individual officers, for example, sometimes bent the rules on such matters as probationer reporting requirements or against leaving the jurisdiction without judicial authorization. Thus, one source of the amorphousness of probation/parole work is the ability of individual officers to modify the policy of the director as they implement that policy.

Another source of the amorphous nature of the job lies in Studt's (1973) description of the officer as a jack-of-all-trades who engages in a variety of tasks: counseling (service), monitoring (surveillance), providing information, and brokering. Because every officer juggles and combines these various activities in a unique manner, probation/parole work varies from officer to officer and has been called the "N + 1" profession:

> This juggling, jack-of-all-trades modus operandi did not seem to provide the probation officer with his or her own separate profession but seemed to represent a composite of professions so that we might call probation the *N + 1 Profession.* Probation is an eclectic collectivity of (partial) professions. It is maintaining the composite while remaining humane that is at the essence of the job (Sullivan, Elwin, & Dexter, 1977, pp. 102–3).

To use another of Sullivan, Elwin, and Dexter's metaphors, individual officers add their own flavor or color to their tasks and thereby determine how they as individuals appear to probationers/parolees. The tasks may be prosaic. The tasks, on the surface, may appear to be either helping activities (social work) or controlling (law enforcement) activities. How the officer translates these prosaic or ambiguous activities to the offender determines the precise interpretation of the activities. Thus, as in other jobs, the individual officer fashions the job.

The ability of the individual line worker to articulate the job is not unlimited. On the one hand, there are formal limits such as statutes, court decisions, and official policies. On the other hand, there are informal pressures to protect the office from negative publicity and upper management scrutiny (McCleary, 1978). Yet, in the final analysis, the officer does exercise a great deal of discretion concerning how the job is done.

THE WORKLOAD AS A SOURCE OF BURNOUT

In his model of the burnout process, Cherniss (1980) noted that the first stage of the process is an imbalance between demands and resources. In probation or parole, this imbalance can take the form of too many clients or too many investigations to perform. Excessive contact with clients is also considered an important source of burnout in Maslach's (1976) model. One federal study of probation, for example, reported that the average caseload for officers in the four jurisdictions studied was 85 probationers per officer, compared with an ideal caseload of 35 probationers per officer (General Accounting Office, 1976). Because officers in these jurisdictions also had to conduct presentence investigations, the report concluded that "probationers are not closely supervised or provided necessary services" (General Accounting Office, 1976, p. 40).

This conclusion, however, assumes that all offenders are similar and, therefore, need equal amounts or intensities of supervision. It also assumes that officers attempt to give equal amounts or intensities of supervision. An alternative model is that there are high-success potential or low-need offenders who require less supervision than low-success potential or high-need offenders (Carter, Glaser, & Wilkins, 1976). In such a more complex model of supervision, caseload size can vary according to the type of offender one supervises. Thus, an officer with 85 low-need offenders may be facing approximately the same pressures as an officer with 35 high-need offenders. In summary, caseload size alone probably has some upper limit that becomes stress inducing; even 200 low-need offenders may be too many to monitor. However, the type of offender one supervises can make a critical difference; therefore, it is simplistic to expect caseload size alone to be a source of burnout. Accordingly, caseload will be one of the factors, but not the only factor, examined later in this report.

Cherniss (1980a, 1980b) has also contended that human service workers seek to be competent and effective, but that this pursuit is elusive because clients do not supply feedback that demonstrates success. More fundamentally, there may be a problem of client resistance or lack of motivation so that positive feedback becomes impossible because positive feedback presumes interaction. These difficulties have been observed in probation and parole work. Ohlin, Piven, and Pappenfort (1956), for example, have noted the reality shock of new officers in experiencing a discrepancy between their expectations of clients as willing, motivated, and able and the reality of uncooperative, if not hostile, offenders. Both Irwin (1970) and McCleary (1978) have noted the tendency of parolees to prefer officers who are minimally intrusive. In fact,

> if a parolee sees his parole officer walking down the street, the parolee changes course and speed so as to evade the parole officer. The parole officer is indeed a significant other in the parolee's social world, but the parolee minimizes his interaction with the parole officer, and hence, never becomes a significant other to the parole officer (McCleary, 1978, p. 164).

In this atmosphere, it is hard to contact offenders and to receive the positive feedback that leads to feelings of competence. Ironically, too much contact can be stressful, but so also can too little contact because it precludes the opportunity to test one's effectiveness. Thus, lack of contact may be a relief from stress, or it may engender stress.

THE ORGANIZATIONAL DESIGN AS A SOURCE OF BURNOUT

Problems in organizational design — the formal, rational, and changeable properties of an organization (Cherniss, 1980b) — are one of the major sources of burnout. One problematic aspect of organizational design is role conflict. One form of role conflict is person-role conflict; one's values are in conflict with role requirements or expectations. For example, an officer trained as a social worker may feel that "the only genuine guarantee of community protection lies in the client's personal adjustment since external conformity will be only temporary. . . . The diagnostic categories and treatment skills which he employs stem from an objective and theoretically based assessment of the client's situation, needs, and capacities" (Ohlin, Piven, & Pappenfort, 1956, p. 215). Problems can arise, however, because other workers, supervisors, judges, police authorities, and the community may have expectations of the worker that differ from the therapeutic expectation internalized in college. For example, a supervisor may urge an officer to revoke probation on the grounds of a new arrest for a minor charge or because of a temporary absconding from the jurisdiction. The officer with a social work background may interpret the violating behavior as "acting out," which is a problematic but necessary state of growth. Hence, conflict arises that can be a source of stress leading to burnout.

One adaptation to this conflict is for the worker to assume a welfare role adaptation and emphasize the skills learned in college. In the punitive role adaptation, the officer would emphasize compliance with middle-class morality by using threats and punishment to control the offender and thereby protect the community. In the protective role adaptation, an agent would vacillate between an emphasis on protecting the community and assisting the offender (Ohlin, Piven, & Pappenfort, 1956).

Given the growth of criminal justice programs in colleges and universities, it is possible that fewer workers are entering the field with an internalized treatment orientation. Thus, role conflict as person-role conflict may be less of a problem today than it was in 1956, but intersender role conflict may still be a problem. The term intersender conflict refers to the situation in which others in one's role set are sending conflicting messages to the focal person (Cherniss, 1980; Katz & Kahn, 1978). A particular probation director, for example, may be committed to a punishment philosophy whereas the probationer may be asking for assistance and special favors.

The conflict arises because the focal person or role incumbent (the officer) has to attempt to reconcile these conflicting expectations. In the literature, this type of conflict usually has been seen as conflict between treatment and punishment, but it need not be limited to only that type of conflict. For example, it may involve mundane matters such as a director who stipulates that clients be quiet and not eat in the waiting room whereas the clients may feel that portable radios and snack foods are legitimate aids to pass the time. Whatever his/her correctional philosophy, the probation officer can be caught in the middle of such conflicting expectations; he must decide to monitor the queue in the waiting room or to make the waiting experience more palatable.

Much of the literature on probation and parole subsequent to the pioneering work of Ohlin and his colleagues has continued to focus on the conflict between an emphasis on treatment and an emphasis on control. Miles (1965), for example, found this sort of conflict to be problematic for Wisconsin probation officers, especially new officers with social work training. With experience, however, the officer resolved the dilemma "by recognizing that his primary responsibility is the protection of society" (Miles, 1965, p. 21). Glaser (1969) has developed a four-fold typology of role adaptations depending on an individual's emphasis on assistance versus his/her emphasis on control. Officers scoring high on both assistance and control aspects are called paternal; those low on control and high on assistance are categorized as welfare officers; those low on assistance but high on control are labeled punitive officers; those low on both dimensions are called passive officers. Arguably, paternal officers are the most likely candidates for burnout because they are trying to emphasize two conflicting concerns. Both welfare and punitive officers would be under stress if their agency emphasized the policy directly opposed to their own. However, if agency policy is congruent with their adaptation, then they should not be under stress. Passive officers would seem to be already burned out or impervious to burnout if they are just avoiding the battle.

Pownal (1963), Klockars (1972), and Tomaino (1975) have offered similar typologies, whereas Studt (1973) has labeled the problem a conflict between surveillance and service. Importantly, she notes that the technology of parole is more surveillance than service oriented because the techniques available to officers are actually surveillance "tools" rather than service "tools." For example, officers are instructed to make surprise visits on parolees. The lack of notice, however, means that the parolee is not ready for a serious discussion and for the development of a problem-solving relationship. Instead, the parolee feels that he/she has been checked on.

Others have offered possible solutions to the conflict. Conrad (1973, 1982, 1984), for example, has suggested that the conflict can be eliminated or reduced by assigning the surveillance function to the police. Probation officers (or perhaps a private agency) would provide services. A recent variation of Conrad's proposal is Rosecrance's (1986) suggestion that probation officers provide neither service nor surveillance but instead function only as report writers for the courts. Barkdull (1976) and Fogel, McAnany, and Thomson (1980) have argued that the probation officer should focus on making probation tougher than it has been by enforcing the conditions of probation and by devoting more attention to the victims of crime. Such attention to victim concerns is part of a justice model of probation. In a related vein, Clear and O'Leary (1983, 1984) have argued that officers should focus on risk control; that is, they should suggest and enforce probation conditions that incapacitate probationers. A curfew would be an example of such a probation condition in their model. Others have suggested that the problems arising from an excessive or unrealistic emphasis on treatment can be resolved by reconceptualizing the role of the officer from that of a therapist to that of a service broker (Dell'Apa, Adams, Jorgensen, & Sigurdson, 1976) or a case manager (Dietrich, 1979). Because these roles do not involve direct counseling, they are less likely to cause a problem if the officer is forced to initiate a violation of probation or some other enforcement action.

It is doubtful that any change will eliminate the conflict between assistance and control, service and surveillance in community corrections. The conflict has been mentioned in the literature so often precisely because it is inherent in the job. Probation and parole are attempts to provide assistance and to maintain some level of control over offenders. To exert that the issue is a "sham" issue, as Thomson and Fogel (1980) have done, does not resolve the dilemma. More honest is the admission that the conflict is inherent in probation and parole and must be confronted.

Professional-Bureaucratic Role Conflict

Because officers work in public agencies rather than as private practice professionals like lawyers, professional-bureaucratic role conflict can arise in probation and parole. As public employees, officers are employed in bureaucratic organizations that stress "orderliness, standardization, uniformity, efficiency, public accountability, and impersonality" (Cherniss, 1980b, p. 86). Such agency priorities can conflict with a professional service ideal, often learned in college, that focuses on "the uniqueness of the individual, sensitivity to the special needs of each client, flexibility, individual initiative and resourcefulness, and the goal of personal growth and development" (Cherniss, 1980b, p. 86).

A concrete example of such conflict in probation is agency emphasis on presentence investigation work and other paperwork instead of on the supervision of probationers and parolees. Both Glaser (1969) and McCleary (1978) found such agency concentration on paperwork whereas officers preferred more time for direct contact with offenders. This can be a source of burnout for a worker socialized to the role of a human service provider because "many of the tasks they are required to perform, such as paperwork, are part of a 'bureaucratic self-image' that is regarded as inferior and limits their opportunities to engage in 'real' work. When this occurs, the worker feels unfulfilled and is likely to become frustrated and impatient" (Cherniss, 1980b, pp. 155–56).

Blumberg (1979), however has offered a different interpretation. He sees probation presentence reports as not mere "paperwork" but as potentially completely professional diagnostic tools:

> To arrive at a diagnosis the worker uses raw material and data about the client gleaned from other social agencies, relatives, friends, schools, employers, public records, medical records, and any other

> such sources as may be available. He then interprets and analyzes the information and decides upon the nature of the client's problems and their probable solutions. Diagnosis and classification based on intimate knowledge of the client's personality are central to what has been called the diagnostic school of social work (Blumberg, 1979, p. 269).

Several factors, however, detract from the potentially professional character of presentence work. First, although authorities suggest that an officer conduct no more than 12 investigations a month, actual assignments often involve 18 to 20 investigations a month. Second, most investigations are clear-cut; there is little question about the eventual sentence, and the officer does not really need to conduct an elaborate investigation. In response, officers may just copy old reports (many offenders are repeat offenders). Third, judges often ignore the reports and instead base their sentencing decisions on the offender's previous record. In the end, the presentence investigation process is not a professional task but an instance of "cooling out" the "mark," of feigning personal concern for the defendant so that he/she offers information that will be of use to the court. The offender thinks that contrite confession will assist his/her cause; the officer is concerned about organizational ends such as perpetuating the organization and preventing unfavorable publicity.

Gilsinan (1982) agrees with Blumberg that many cases are routine — the defendant clearly deserves either incarceration or probation. Other cases, however, are more controversial; different probation officers have varying opinions about "the kind of person they like to see on probation" (Gilsinan, 1982, p. 181). These cases add interest to what is often a routine task.

In conclusion, reports clearly can be time consuming and routine and possibly conflict with an officer's desire to engage in more professional activities such as individual or group counseling sessions with offenders. As such, paperwork can be a source of job stress leading to burnout for officers. However, investigations can also be satisfying. The investigator may take seriously the notion that presentence reports are supposed to be diagnostic reports or may consider them to be thorough, though not necessarily diagnostic, investigations of the defendant's background. Several officers known to the writer take pride in conducting painstakingly complete investigations into the backgrounds of the offenders they investigate. Contrary to Blumberg's (1979) charge, these investigators are not perverse voyeurs who achieve vicarious satisfaction by examining the relatively exotic lives of offenders. Rather, they simply desire to do a job and to do it well; they relish the sense of accomplishment evident in a well-done report over the often invisible rewards of supervising probationers or parolees. After a month of conducting investigations, one can point to some finished products. After a month of supervising offenders, one may have difficulty pointing to even one concrete accomplishment.

Studt (1973) has provided further evidence of professional-bureaucratic conflict in probation and parole. On the one hand, almost all the officers she studied noted impatience with "red tape" and "meaningless" directives and a feeling of lack of recognition: "As in most bureaucracies, these bottom level workers felt unrecognized and unappreciated by upper administration; in the agents' view the people 'at the top' had little awareness of the real nature of the agent's job" (Studt, 1973, p. 41). In addition to lack of recognition, the problem can be one of lack of involvement in agency policy making; "one of the major problems has been the relative isolation of the front-line staff from the formulation and elaboration of policy at the upper organizational levels and the attempts by management to implement unilaterally newer policies without interacting with front-line personnel in any significant way (Duffee, 1980, p. 238).

A recent study (Thomson & Fogel, 1980) of training provision and needs in small probation agencies (agencies with fewer than ten workers) has shed additional light on the issues of probation officers' desires for professionalism in the face of bureaucratic practices. In order, the officers noted these problems: amount of paperwork, lack of community resources, caseload size, travel distances, lack of public support, lack of interagency cooperation, lack of office space or equipment, and lack of secretarial help (Thomson & Fogel, 1980). These problems frustrate officers in their desire to effect changes in probationers and thereby inhibit feelings of competence and professionalism.

Hagan (1975) offered an interesting note related to the possibility of professional-bureaucratic conflict when he remarked that the presentence investigation is actually "dirty work" in the terminology of Everett Hughes. That is, collecting information on defendants is necessary but unclean or unpleasant. The officer has to sit down with criminals to get the information. This dirty work, however, can be elevated in status or rendered "professional" if the officers are offered "prestige conferring opportunities to offer pre-sentence recommendations. The results of these organizational arrangements, then, may be socially rewarding for both groups" (Hagan, 1975, p. 623). Based on this, it would appear that probation agencies that allow the officer to make recommendations would be more professionally oriented and, therefore, less stressful for officers than would be probation departments that do not allow the officer to make sentence recommendations.

In summary, professional-bureaucratic role conflict has been cited as a possible source of burnout, and evidence in the probation and parole literature shows that such conflict does exist in the field.

Role Ambiguity

A second aspect of the organizational design of a probation or parole agency that can contribute to burnout is role ambiguity or the lack of "the information necessary for adequate performance of the role" (Cherniss, 1980b, p. 89). Perhaps the most fundamental ambiguity problem in probation and parole is the "paucity of available knowledge and techniques concerning intervention with offenders" (Ohlin, Piven, & Pappenfort, 1956, p. 217). As the recent Panel on Research on Rehabilitative Techniques concluded, "there is not now in the scientific literature any basis for any policy or recommendations regarding rehabilitation of criminal offenders" (Sechrest,

White, & Brown, 1979, p. 34). Thus, there is considerable doubt concerning the ability of officers to effect changes in the lives of offenders that will help them to avoid crime.

Another source of role ambiguity in probation and parole is that the goals are often ambiguous. Departments often attempt to achieve some undefined combination of retribution, deterrence, incapacitation, and rehabilitation. Such a hodgepodge of ill-defined goals creates role ambiguity for individual officers that can lead to burnout.

A third source of role ambiguity is that performance criteria are ambiguous. At first glance, it might seem that this should not be a problem in probation and parole because the traditional measure of success in corrections has been recidivism (Sechrest, White, & Brown, 1979). A focus on recidivism as a performance measure, however, is not without problems. First, there are various definitions of recidivism, for example, dichotomous versus continuous and arrest versus reconviction. Second, even if agreement can be reached on a definition, the measurement of recidivism is difficult because offenders are often transient and may be hard to monitor. They may recidivate in a new locale, unbeknown to the tracking agency. Third, conscientious officers who work hard to detect and report infractions may be considered unsuccessful because the recidivism rates for their caseloads are high. Fourth, there are many factors affecting client behavior, and it may be unrealistic to expect officers to have a significant influence on recidivism (Polisky, 1981b). In response to these difficulties, some (Polisky, 1981b; Waller, 1974) have suggested that measurable and attainable goals be set for officers, taking into account the wide range of job activities that officers perform. Offices with more meaningful measures of activity and effectiveness would be less stressful for officers than would be offices that rely on the traditional criterion of recidivism.

SUPPORT AND BURNOUT

Burnout writers have argued that support from supervisors and colleagues helps to prevent burnout (Cherniss, 1980b; Maslach, 1976). Supervisors can be supportive by providing technical assistance, emotional support, feedback, advocacy, and responsiveness. Unfortunately, the literature indicates that such supervisory support is often lacking in probation and parole.

Ohlin and his colleagues (1956) have related the lack of support to the previously discussed issue of role conflict. Specifically, an officer with a role orientation differing from management's may feel a lack of support. A treatment oriented worker in a restricted agency focusing on law enforcement concerns might well feel "that the central focus of these supervisors is to prevent him from acting in ways which might embarrass the agency. He feels that treatment problems not involving the possibility of public condemnation are of secondary concern and that aiding his professional growth very seldom becomes a work function" (Ohlin, Piven, & Pappenfort, 1956, p. 219).

Sullivan, Elwin, and Dexter (1977, p. 71) have argued that probation supervisors are not supportive mentors but rather bureaucratic "checkers":

"The supervisor is a supervisor. He monitors the work of the probation officer essentially to see to it that the work of the probation officer stays within prescribed, although frequently unstated, organizational norms. He reserves the power to modify." Such monitoring usually focuses on written products such as the presentence report, case folders, revocation requests, and daily activity reports to insure that the officers adhere to agency format. It is difficult to see such "checkers," who allow no autonomy for officers, as significant sources of support.

Like Sullivan, McCleary (1978) found that supervisors checked the written reports of parole officers, but the concern was compliance with informal norms rather than format. This meant that if the officers did whatever was necessary to assist supervisors "to run their offices in an efficient and trouble-free manner" (McCleary, 1978, p. 57), then the officers could expect a high degree of freedom to cut office hours, to be extremely autonomous about field visits, and to have their written reports approved. In summary, McCleary (1978) has contended that the parole supervisors he studied were supportive of officers when they helped to maintain a smooth-running branch office team free of interference from upper management in the central office. The reason for this was that supervisors were middle men with superiors of their own. The supervisors had to handle the expectations, often contradictory, of their superiors and of their officers. Similarly, even probation directors must deal with the expectations of judges, county legislators, and state regulatory agencies. Thus, often supervisors cannot be completely supportive of officers because they are located in such middle-management positions.

Colleague support, whether in the form of emotional support, technical support, or group unity vis-à-vis management, is also an important preventive or ameliorative weapon against burnout (Cherniss, 1980a, 1980b; Maslach, 1976, 1982). The probation and parole literature is unclear about the extent of such collegial support but suggests that it is at least possible in the job.

Studt (1973) reported that the parole officers she studied were engrossed with extrawork concerns such as the stock market, politics, or getting an advanced degree and that they "did not talk much among themselves about these interests" (Studt, 1973, p. 40). This apparent lack of support contrasts with McCleary's (1978) depiction of another parole agency with two cliques: the professionals and the veterans. The veterans were the older officers who were not college graduates but who obtained their jobs through political patronage whereas the professionals were younger, college-educated officers who shared an ideology that emphasized "the importance of the client, the therapeutic ideal and related concerns" (McCleary, 1978, p. 71). There appeared to be support within these cliques; the professionals, for example, socialized after work on a regular basis. Similarly, there appeared to be support across the two groups in that potentially disruptive incidents were resolved to safeguard the greater good of the entire branch office team.

Thus it appears that support is variable from agency to agency and that officers in supportive agencies may be experiencing less frequent feelings of burnout than their counterparts in less supportive settings.

CONCLUSION

This review of the literature on the employment conditions of probation and parole officers shows that there are several problems in the field. Much of the literature has focused on the role conflict between assistance and control. Justice model writers such as Fogel and Thomson (1980) and risk control model writers (O'Leary & Clear, 1984) have argued that the decades-long debate over such conflict has been misguided and that attention should turn to increased concern for the victim and for public protection. Yet one wonders if new clothes can cover up a problem that has been discussed so persistently. More tangible are the problems of high caseloads, excessive paperwork, lack of resources in the community to address offender needs, resistant clients, and the extent of supervisory support for line officers.

Given these problems and given the research and writing on burnout to date, it is reasonable to suspect that burnout is problematic for some officers. To determine the extent of the problem and to examine the specific sources of the problem in probation and parole, a survey instrument was assembled and sent to a sample of officers and managers. Details of the study methodology are presented in the next chapter.

Methodology 5

This chapter describes the sampling procedure and questionnaire construction for the study of burnout in probation and parole officers, which was the initial focus of the study. As detailed below, this portion of the research involved responses from almost 1,000 probation and parole personnel in four states. This chapter also discusses the demographic characteristics of the sample and descriptive findings on the levels of burnout.

This chapter also lays the groundwork for the subsequent discussions of the causes of burnout (Chapter 6), gender differences in burnout (Chapter 7), managerial versus line officer burnout (Chapter 8), and a qualitative analysis of the open-ended comments of the respondents about burnout (Chapter 9).

This chapter does not discuss, however, the methodological issues surrounding the second round of the research. As noted in Chapter 1, Maslach's burnout items were administered at a second time to a sample of both probation/parole and correctional officers in Alabama. The methodological aspects and findings of that replication and extension of the original probation/parole research are presented in Chapter 10.

SAMPLING PROCEDURE

The original intention for the research for this study was to secure a national sample of federal probation and parole officers. When the national director did not consent to participate in the research, a sample of officers in New York State and in Indiana was chosen. The author was working in Indiana at the time and had worked previously in New York. Several contacts in those two states agreed to allow the officers in their departments to participate in the study. In this sense, the original sampling decision was a convenience sample. Once these states were chosen, however, it was decided to attempt to include every probation office in the two states and each parole division office in Indiana. Shortly after this decision had been made, administrators in one federal office, the Eastern District of Pennsylvania, and in the Adult Probation Office of the State of Connecticut agreed to allow their personnel to participate in the study.

The New York State Division of Parole initially declined to participate in the research but then consented. By that time, however, practical considerations such as cost precluded the inclusion of New York Parole.

Specifically, when the New York State Parole Division finally agreed to participate, planning indicated that about 1,500 questionnaires would have to be mailed out to all those who had consented to participate in the research. The addition of New York parole officers at that late date would have strained both financial resources[1] and practical resources relating to the author's ability to coordinate data collection and analysis. Thus, due to tardy consent, New York parole personnel were not included in the research.

Sample Sites

The inclusion of officers and managerial personnel from Connecticut, Indiana, New York, and part of Pennsylvania ensured that the survey would include subjects from diverse areas of the country and from different types of correctional organizations. Geographically, the sample included a New England state, a middle Atlantic state, a midwestern state, and the Philadelphia region. Thus, sample sites ranged from big city offices to small, rural departments. Organizationally, the sample ranged from large, bureaucratic departments with a specialized, pyramidal structure to "departments" of one officer acting as a generalist jack-of-all-trades officer.

At the time of the survey, probation in New York operated within the executive branch of county government and was thus technically, though not operationally, independent of the judiciary. That is, day-to-day interaction often led to cooperation with, if not cooptation by, the judges, as often occurs with public defenders (Blumberg, 1979). In addition, a state executive branch office, the New York State Division of Probation, assisted the county probation departments "in providing services through rules, financial support, direct services, training, data collection, and general supervision" (American Correctional Association, 1981, p. 292). To fulfill these objectives, the state established training programs for officers, contributed about 40 percent of the funding necessary for operating the local departments, and provided consultants to offer advice and monitor compliance with state directives. At the time of the survey, the state also actually operated the local probation departments in three small counties. This was supposed to be the precursor of an eventual state takeover of probation from the counties, but that change never took place.

Probation in Indiana at the time of the survey was also a local function, although it was a judicial function rather than an executive function as in New York. As a judicial function, officers were under the ultimate authority of a judge: "Probation officers shall serve at the pleasure of the appointing court and are directly responsible to and subject to the orders of the court" (Indiana Code 11-13-1, cited in Indiana Judicial Conference, 1982, p. 9). Additionally, the Indiana Judicial Center, the staff agency for the Indiana Judicial Conference (consisting of all full-time judges in the state) was responsible for certification, training, and standards development (National Council on Crime and Delinquency, 1981). Evidence of the local nature of probation in Indiana is the fact that the Judicial Center did not begin operations until 1981. The first statewide conference of officers was not held until 1982.

In contrast, parole in Indiana was a state function administered by the Department of Corrections through the Community Services Division. Eight district parole offices served the state's 92 counties. Each district had a district supervisor comparable to a county probation director or chief probation officer. The districts employed fewer than 20 officers each.

In Connecticut, adult probation supervision operated as a state agency administered by the Judicial Department of the unified State Superior Court system. Technically, probation could not be a county function because "county" is only a geographical term in the state, not a unit of government. The Department of Adult Probation established four district, regional offices with a total of 16 suboffices in the four districts (American Correctional Association, 1981).

The federal officers in the sample were employed in the Eastern District of Pennsylvania and served ten counties in the eastern region of the state. They worked out of offices in Philadelphia and Reading. These officers were both probation officers for the federal district courts and parole officers for the federal correctional institutions. Because the chief judge exercised control by choosing a probation director, in a sense, these officers were more local employees than federal employees. They did not take a national civil service test but were hired at the discretion of the local director.

Sampling

In New York and Indiana, county directors and chief probation officers, respectively, were contacted requesting permission to survey personnel in the county departments. Sixty-two percent of the directors in New York State and 65 percent of the chief probation officers in Indiana agreed to participate. Questionnaires were sent to all of the officers in the participating counties and to all officers in Connecticut, Indiana parole, and the Eastern District of Pennsylvania. In the majority of cases, questionnaires were sent to the director/chief probation officer who distributed the questionnaires to the employees. Each employee received a questionnaire, a cover letter, and a stamped envelope addressed to the author so that employers had no access to the responses of the workers.

A minority of the respondents received their questionnaires directly in the mail because their director/chief probation officer had provided a list of employees. Although it would have been preferable to send all the questionnaires in this manner, allowing directors the option of choosing either method of distribution was chosen in the expectation that directors would be more likely to participate if given such a choice.

Response Rate

Overall, 1,517 questionnaires were sent in July 1981, and 968 questionnaires were returned. Table 5.1 shows the specific breakdowns by sample site.

TABLE 5.1
Survey Response Rates

Subsample	Questionnaires Mailed	Number Returned	Response Rate
New York State	888	556	63%
Indiana Probation	384	262	68%
Indiana Parole	40	30	75%
Connecticut	160	87	54%
Philadelphia	45	33	73%
Total	1,517	968	64%

The overall response rate of 64 percent is midway between what Babbie (1986) considers "good" (60 percent) and "better" (70 percent). This response rate was achieved with a limited follow-up mailing — 61 directors (those in the departments with the lowest response rates) were sent a letter four to six weeks after the initial mailing requesting them to remind their employees about the questionnaire. Only a limited follow-up was conducted because most directors had chosen a bulk mailing of questionnaires to themselves for distribution to their employees and because code numbers were not used in an effort to emphasize the anonymity of the research.

Sample Representativeness

The sample is more clearly representative of probation than of parole officers. Only Indiana parole officers and one federal probation and parole office were included in the sample. Most of the respondents were probation officers exclusively. Thus, the findings reported below are more applicable to probation officers than they are to parole officers. This does not mean that the findings have no applicability to parole officers. Because some states follow the federal practice of combining the two functions and because textbooks often treat probation and parole as more similar than different (see, e.g., Allen, Eskridge, Latessa, & Vito, 1985; Carter, Glaser, & Wilkins, 1984; Hussey & Duffee, 1980), findings about probation officers have significant relevance for parole officers.

Another way to look at the representativeness of the sample is to compare it with other samples of probation workers. For example, a comparison of the study sample (line officers only; N = 711) with a sample of Canadian probation officers (N = 255) studied by Cjapo and Clarke (1976) showed important similarities. Workers in both samples had very similar levels of education and experience; specifically, almost 100 percent of both samples were college educated and over 50 percent in each sample had less than 15 years experience. More of the Canadian officers, however, were male (89 percent versus 60 percent) and under 30 (50 percent versus 38 percent) (Cjapo & Clarke, 1976) compared with U.S. workers. Table 5.2 shows a comparison of the study sample with the sample of officers in small agencies (agencies with fewer than 10 officers) mentioned earlier (Thomson & Fogel, 1980). Examination of Table 5.2 shows that the two samples are very similar except in gender: 82 percent of the Thomson-Fogel respondents were male, but only 63 percent of the study sample was male. Given the caution that the Thomson-Fogel sample consisted of workers only in small agencies, the similarities between the two samples suggest that the study sample is not grossly divergent from another recent, sizable sample of probation workers. Given this finding and given the fact that the study sample was drawn from probation departments in three states and totaled almost 1,000 respondents, it seems safe to conclude that the sample is fairly representative of probation officers in the states studied and in other states sharing essential characteristics with the study states. Most important, the sample is an improvement over many previous burnout study samples gathered at conventions or workshops with response rates around 30 percent (Ursprung, 1986).

QUESTIONNAIRE CONSTRUCTION

The Maslach Burnout Inventory was used to measure the dependent variable, burnout.[2] Factor analysis (Maslach & Jackson, 1981) has indicated that this 25-item inventory measures three aspects of burnout. The first

TABLE 5.2
Comparison of Study Sample and Thomson-Fogel Sample of Officers in Small Agencies

Characteristic	Study Sample	Thomson-Fogel Sample
Percent male	63%	82%
Percent white	95%	93%
Median age	33	33
Percent under age 30	32%	28%
Percent line officers	71%	74%
Experience	49%[a]	54%[b]
n	968	1094

Note: Thomson-Fogel sample data are found in Thomson & Fogel (1980, pp. 131–36).
[a]Percent with less than 5 years of experience.
[b]Percent with 5 years or less of experience.

factor or subscale of the inventory, labeled the emotional exhaustion subscale, describes "feelings of being emotionally overextended and exhausted by one's work" (Maslach & Jackson, 1981, p. 101). Nine items constitute the scale; the item with the highest loading on this factor directly asks the respondents about their level of burnout. The depersonalization factor comprises five items that describe an unfeeling or impersonal approach to clients, such as treating clients like objects or becoming more callous since taking the job (Maslach & Jackson, 1981).

Eight items make up the third factor, the personal accomplishment subscale, which describes "feelings of competence and successful achievement in one's work with people" (Maslach & Jackson, 1981, p. 101). Items address such issues as dealing with problems in a calm fashion and exerting some influence on clients' lives.

A fourth factor, involvement, appeared, but its eigenvalue was less than unity. Originally, Maslach called this an optional subscale, but later she dropped the three items constituting the factor and renamed her questionnaire the Human Services Inventory (a 22-item inventory). Table 5.3 lists sample items from the Burnout Inventory.

Following Maslach, all items were measured on seven-point frequency (ranging from never to everyday) and intensity scales (ranging from very mild, barely noticeable to very strong, major). If a person answered "never" (0) on the frequency scale, a score of zero was assigned on the intensity dimension. Subsequent research (see, e.g., Golembiewski, Munzenrider, & Stevenson, 1986) has found that the two dimensions correlate to such an extent that measurement of the frequency dimension alone is sufficient. High scores on the emotional exhaustion and depersonalization scales indicate high levels of burnout; high scores on the personal accomplishment scale indicate low burnout.

Two modifications were made in the administration of the Maslach Burnout Inventory. First, the items read "probationer-parolees," where

TABLE 5.3
Sample Maslach Burnout Inventory Items

1. I feel emotionally drained from my work.
2. I feel used up at the end of the workday.
3. I feel fatigued when I get up in the morning and have to face another day on the job.
4. I can easily understand how my recipients feel about things.
5. I feel I treat some recipients as if they were impersonal objects.

Note: Reproduced by special permission of the publisher, Consulting Psychologists Press, Inc., Palo Alto, CA 94306, from Maslach Burnout Survey — Human Services Survey by Christina Maslach/Susan E. Jackson, copyright 1981. Further reproduction is prohibited without the publisher's consent.

applicable, instead of "recipients." Similar modifications have proven to have no detrimental effect on the measurement properties of the inventory (Iwanicki & Schwab, 1981). Second, six additional items measuring intrinsic job satisfaction were interspersed throughout the 25 burnout items in an attempt to test the discriminant validity of the personal accomplishment items.

Factor Analysis of the Burnout Items

Factor analysis (principal factoring with iteration and an orthogonal [varimax] rotation) of the burnout items for the probation/parole employees indicated support for Maslach and Jackson's (1981) four-factor solution, but there were some discrepancies. When the selection criterion for the number of factors was percent of the variance explained, the factor analysis was very consistent with that of Maslach and Jackson, except for a few minor variations that could be accounted for by random error and did not warrant a revision of her scales. That is, when the criterion for choosing the number of factors was to stop at factors that explained at least 5 percent of the variance, four factors resulted. Moreover, the factor loadings of the respective items were very similar to those obtained by Maslach and Jackson. However, Maslach and Jackson used the criterion of eigenvalue greater than one to obtain their four-factor solution. That criterion resulted in a five-factor solution for the probation employee data (for a further discussion of these issues, see Kim & Mueller, 1978a, 1978b). Furthermore, as discussed in a later section, inclusion of intrinsic job satisfaction items indicated that two (and almost three) of the satisfaction items were very closely related to what Maslach and Jackson have called personal accomplishment.

To sum up, a four-factor solution of the burnout items was consistent with the solution of Maslach and Jackson (1981). However, to obtain that particular solution, a criterion (explaining at least 5 percent of the variance) had to be used that was different from the one Maslach and Jackson used (eigenvalue greater than one). Nevertheless, given the consistency of one four-factor solution and given the desire to compare the burnout scores of the probation/parole workers with scores presented by Maslach and Jackson, it was decided to agree with Maslach and Jackson that the data supported a four-factor solution. Thus, the emotional exhaustion, depersonalization, and personal accomplishment scores reported throughout this research include the same items used by Maslach and Jackson (1981). As explained later in this chapter, however, the research on the probation and parole employees indicates that the accomplishment factor is problematic.

Reliability Findings

Coefficient alpha was computed for the entire Burnout Inventory and for the separate subscales. The coefficients were higher than those found by Maslach and Jackson (1981) in their data from human service workers. Specifically, for the officer data, coefficient alpha for the entire inventory was .83 for the frequency dimension and .86 for the intensity dimension. The subscale coefficients ranged from a low of .83 for the depersonalization scales (frequency and intensity) to a high of .92 for the exhaustion scale (frequency dimension). Thus, the complete inventory and its subscales are very reliable measures.

Other Measures

In addition to demographic items on age, sex, race, and so forth, various job, organizational, and attitudinal questions were included in the questionnaire. Some of these are detailed here; some of the more important items are reported verbatim in subsequent chapters (see especially Chapter 8).

Client contact was measured by asking the workers how many hours they spent in face-to-face contact with probationers during a typical week. This question was a modified version of the client contact question in the Maslach Burnout Inventory and was included because of the centrality of client contact to burnout in Maslach's model (see Chapter 3). Caseload was used as another measure of the demands confronting officers; it was calculated by summing the number of adult supervision cases and juvenile cases officers were handling in a typical month. Officers were also asked how many investigations and intake cases they handled in a typical month.

The job satisfaction measure was the measure of intrinsic job satisfaction used in *The 1977 Quality of Employment Survey* (Quinn & Staines, 1979) to reflect "a worker's desire to be stimulated and challenged by his or her job and to be able to exercise acquired skills at work" (Quinn & Staines, 1979, p. 212). The actual items are:

> The work is interesting.
> I have an opportunity to develop my own special abilities.
> I can see the results of my work.
> I am given a chance to do the things I do best.
> I am given a lot of freedom to decide how to do my own work.
> The problems I am expected to solve are hard enough (Quinn & Staines, 1979, pp. 216–17).

All six items were included in the probation/parole questionnaire and were used in the factor analysis of Maslach's Burnout items to determine if there is any significant relationship between the personal accomplishment aspect of burnout and satisfaction (see the next section of this chapter). Five of the items were used to create an intrinsic job satisfaction scale (used in the path analysis reported in Chapter 6) and showed a reliability score (alpha) of .71. One item (the last item listed above) was omitted because it correlated very poorly with the other items. The intrinsic satisfaction items were measured on the same seven-point frequency and intensity dimensions as the burnout items.

Two measures of overall satisfaction with one's career and one's agency were created for this study. They were measured on five-point disagree-agree scales. Their wording and frequency distributions are noted in Chapter 8 in the comparison of managerial and line personnel.

Participation in decision making was measured by a three-item scale (e.g., "Superiors try to get ideas and opinions from officers before making decisions"). Each item was measured on a five-point scale ranging from strongly disagree (1) to strongly agree (5); the scale score noted in Chapter 6 is the mean of the three items. Cronbach's alpha for the scale was .64.

Role conflict was measured by four items used in *The 1977 Quality of Employment Survey* (Quinn & Staines, 1979, p. 196). One item ("I have too much work to do everything well"), however, was modified to "Given the level of resources in this office, some of my tasks just cannot be done well" because this rephrasing was considered more appropriate for probation workers. The four items used to construct the scale used in Chapter 6 were measured on the previously described disagree-agree scale; the scale score noted in Chapter 6 is the mean of the four items. Alpha for the scale was rather low, .49, but the previous use of the scale items in a national sample allowed for some comparison with the responses of workers in other occupations.

The Personal Accomplishment Factor Controversy

As noted, Maslach and Jackson (1981) contend that their personal accomplishment scale is a measure of a "third aspect of the burnout syndrome . . . the tendency to evaluate oneself negatively, particularly with regard to one's work with clients. Workers feel unhappy about themselves and dissatisfied with their accomplishments on the job" (Maslach & Jackson, 1981, p. 1). This description raises the question of the discriminant validity of this subscale versus the concept of intrinsic job satisfaction. Katz and Kahn (1978), for example, define intrinsic job satisfaction as "satisfaction from the content of the work itself — greater feelings of autonomy, of responsibility, of demonstrating one's worth. . . . The assumption is that the challenge of the job motivates people toward greater effort" (Katz & Kahn, 1978, pp. 417–18). The similarity in these definitions — evaluating oneself and one's accomplishments and demonstrating one's worth — led to the inclusion of the previously mentioned six intrinsic job satisfaction items in the questionnaire so that the discriminant validity of the personal accomplishment items versus the satisfaction items could be examined.

Both factor analysis and correlation were used to examine this issue of discriminant validity. When the six satisfaction items were included in an extension factor analysis (see Gorsuch, 1978, for an explanation of this technique) of the 25 burnout items, there appeared to be some slight similarity between the satisfaction items and the personal accomplishment items. Specifically, the six satisfaction items did load positively on the accomplishment factor, but no loadings were above .30. Extension factor analysis, therefore, indicated only slight support for the contention that the concept of personal accomplishment is not distinct from the concept of intrinsic job satisfaction.

As a further test, the intrinsic job satisfaction items were included in a factor analysis of the burnout items. This procedure is different from extension analysis in that it performs the factor analysis on all the respective items as one set of items, whereas extension factor analysis first analyzes the initial items (in this case, the burnout items) and then extends the analysis to the additional items (in this case, the satisfaction items). Two interesting results occurred. First, as hypothesized, there was some relationship between the intrinsic job satisfaction and the personal accomplishment measures. Specifically, two of the intrinsic satisfaction items ("I feel the work is interesting" and "I can see the results of my work") loaded at least .40 on factor two in the rotated factor matrix (actual loadings were .40 and .59, respectively). A third item ("I am given a chance to do the things I do best") just missed the .40 loading criterion; it loaded .39 on factor two. Factor two included five of the Maslach and Jackson accomplishment items. The second noteworthy result was that this factor analysis resulted in a six-factor solution with a splitting of Maslach's personal accomplishment factor into two separate factors. Here one factor appeared to measure accomplishment, and the other appeared to be more of a measure of establishing a relaxed setting for clients. In any case, this factor analysis indicated that three of the intrinsic satisfaction items were closely related to what Maslach and Jackson have called personal accomplishment.

When the satisfaction items and the accomplishment items were combined into mean scores and those scores were correlated, the resulting correlations were .60 on both the frequency and the intensity dimensions. Correlations this high are considerably higher than the correlations of about .20 predicted by Maslach and Jackson (1981) and approach the level of .80, at which many researchers begin to suspect the problem of multicollinearity among independent variables (Lewis-Beck, 1980). Thus, it seems reasonable to infer that although personal accomplishment is not identical to intrinsic job satisfaction, there is considerable similarity between the two concepts. Future research should pay further attention to this issue.

Reasons for Choosing the Maslach Burnout Inventory

There were several reasons for choosing the Maslach Burnout Inventory as the measure of burnout. First, the use of her questionnaire in previous studies of human service workers (Maslach & Jackson, 1981), Social Security workers (Barad, 1979), and prison guards (Schlacter, 1980) allowed for some comparison between the findings in this study and previous findings. Second, the Maslach Burnout Inventory has proven validity and reliability (Maslach & Jackson, 1981). Third, the instrument is a measure of burnout rather than a measure of job dissatisfaction or some other construct that some researchers (e.g., Harrison, 1980) have argued can be used to measure burnout. Fourth, the use of the burnout measure allowed for possible refinement of the measure, particularly those items measuring the aspect of burnout called personal accomplishment.

FINDINGS

Demographic Findings

Seventy-seven percent (N = 746) of the respondents listed their job title as probation officer, parole officer, trainee, aide, or intern. Twenty percent (N = 198) listed their title as probation director, chief probation officer, deputy director, deputy chief probation officer, supervisor, or some other administrative title. The remainder of the respondents described themselves as working in various specialties, such as director of detention or court liaison worker. Most of the respondents reported working in probation departments; only 25 parole officers and 5 district supervisors of the Indiana Parole Department could be considered to be employed in parole work exclusively. The 33 federal employees in the sample could be considered to perform both probation and parole functions.

The sample was predominantly male (63 percent), white (95 percent), and college educated (94 percent had at least a baccalaureate degree). The sample was young to middle-aged; the mean age was 35.7 and the median age was 33. The majority of the respondents (63 percent) were married, but sizable proportions were single (25 percent) or divorced (8 percent). Of those reporting how long they had been married, 78 percent had been married 18 years or less; half had been married nine years or less. The majority (55 percent) reported that they had no children living with them, but 16 percent had one child, and 28 percent had two or more children living with them. As measured by a one-item religiosity indicator, 68 percent of the respondents considered themselves to range from very religious to moderately religious.

More than half (51 percent) of the respondents indicated that they had been employed in probation and parole work for more than five years. However, the sample also included a sizable number of workers (9 percent) who had been on the job a year or less.

Almost half of the respondents (49 percent) indicated that sometime before entering probation or parole they had been employed in human service jobs, such as casework, counseling, teaching, the ministry, or nursing. Given the fact that some writers consider probation officers to have a law enforcement orientation, it was somewhat surprising that only 6 percent of the sample had any previous experience in law enforcement.

There was considerable variation in the size of the agencies in which the employees worked. The two predominant agency sizes were the very small office with one to five officers (reported by 25 percent of the workers) and the office with from 21 to 50 officers (also reported by 25 percent of the respondents). The employees were split almost in half concerning whether officers were generalists responsible for supervision, investigation, and intake functions (reported by 43 percent of the respondents) or specialists limited to only one or two functions (reported by about 54 percent of the respondents).

Extent of Burnout in the Sample

As noted, the Maslach Burnout Inventory items are measured on seven-point frequency and intensity scales. Responses for the frequency dimension range from (0) never to (6) everyday and responses for the intensity dimension range from "very mild, barely noticeable" (1) to "major, very strong" (7). Higher scores represent higher degrees of emotional exhaustion, depersonalization, and personal accomplishment.

Table 5.4 presents the means and standard deviations on the inventory's subscales for the probation/parole workers.

Examination of Table 5.4 shows that the mean burnout scores for the probation/parole employees were not of crisis proportions. On the average, workers were reporting feelings of emotional exhaustion slightly more frequently than once a month and of depersonalization less frequently than once a month. On the positive side, workers were reporting feelings of personal accomplishment about once a week. Thus, burnout was a problem for some but not all workers.

Because Maslach and Jackson (1984b) have published normative data on the burnout scores, it is possible to compare those scores with the scores of the probation/parole employees. Such comparison (z-tests) indicates that the probation/parole workers expressed feelings of emotional exhaustion less frequently than did the sample of human service workers; however, the intensity of feelings of exhaustion was higher for the probation/parole workers. Concerning feelings of depersonalization, officers' scores were similar in terms of frequency but higher than the comparison group in terms of intensity. Similarly, the officers' scores on the personal accomplishment subscale were lower (indicating greater burnout), both in

TABLE 5.4
Mean Burnout Scores for Probation and Parole Employees

	Emotional Exhaustion	Depersonalization	Personal Accomplishment
Frequency			
M	2.29	1.76	4.09
SD	1.16	1.18	0.93
Cases	938	862	845
Intensity			
M	3.57	2.73	4.80
SD	1.42	1.55	0.89
Cases	926	865	837

frequency and intensity, than the comparison group's. In conclusion, the officers were reporting greater burnout than Maslach and Jackson's normative sample of human service workers except for less frequent feelings of emotional exhaustion and similar depersonalization frequency scores.

Another way to examine the data is to review some of the responses to key items. The item directly measuring how burned out workers feel is the item that Maslach and Jackson (1981) reported loaded highest on the factor of emotional exhaustion. The modal response to the frequency dimension of this item for the probation/parole workers was "a few times a year or less." Sixty-two percent of the respondents reported feeling this way only once a month, a few times a year, or never; 13 percent reported feeling this way every day or a few times a week. The item concerning impersonal treatment of clients had the highest factor loading on the scale of depersonalization in Maslach's research. Most probation/parole employees (74 percent) reported that they did not experience this feeling or experienced it only very infrequently. Only about 7 percent of the respondents reported feeling this way once a week or more. The item concerning the worker's ability to deal with emotional problems in a calm manner had the highest factor loading on the subscale of personal accomplishment. Based on this item, officers apparently were experiencing high degrees of personal accomplishment; 67 percent of the workers said that they felt this way a few times a week or everyday. However, the item with the second highest loading on the factor, measuring the worker's influence on other people's lives, had much greater variation in response. Only 41 percent of the workers reported feeling this way a few times a week or everyday, and 47 percent reported feeling such influence on clients' lives only a few times a month or less. Thus it appears that the workers were approaching their jobs very calmly, even though a sizable proportion felt that they only infrequently produced a positive influence on other people's lives through their work.

These findings represent a potpourri of employees from different states and with different job titles. Table 5.5 presents burnout and intrinsic job satisfaction scores for the line probation officers from New York State, Indiana, and Connecticut, Indiana parole officers, and the federal probation and parole line officers from the Eastern District of Pennsylvania. This allows for an examination of line officer burnout scores versus total sample scores, which included managerial personnel (see Chapter 8 for an examination of managerial burnout) and for an examination of agency to agency variation in scores.

Examination of Table 5.5 shows that line officer burnout scores were not very different from the scores for the entire sample (see Table 5.4). This is logical given the extremely high proportion of line officers in the total sample. Review of the table also indicates that Connecticut officers were reporting the highest burnout scores and the lowest satisfaction score in the sample. Although the exhaustion score of the Connecticut officers was not significantly different from officer scores in other agencies, it just missed being statistically significantly different. Scores for workers in other agencies did not differ significantly from one another at the .05 level (Scheffe test).

TABLE 5.5
Mean Burnout and Intrinsic Job Satisfaction Scores by Agency — Line Officers Only

Variable Score	NY POs	IN POs	PA POs	CT POs	IN Parole	All POs
Emotional exhaustion	2.31	2.32	2.47	2.74	2.01	2.34
Depersonalization	1.72	1.75	1.61	2.48[a]	1.85	1.80
Personal accomplishment	4.12	4.28	3.97	3.59[b]	3.93	4.10
Intrinsic job satisfaction	4.14	4.30	3.79	3.56[b]	4.05	4.11

Note: Total *n* varied from 709 to 725; pairwise deletion used.
[a]Connecticut POs differed from NY, IN, & PA POs (Scheffe test).
[b]Connecticut POs differed from NY & IN POs (Scheffe test).
$p < .05$ for Scheffe test comparisons.

DISCUSSION

This examination of the Burnout Inventory subscale scores, and the items with the highest factor loadings on the subscales, leads to several conclusions. With the exceptions of the frequency dimensions of emotional exhaustion and depersonalization, officers reported experiencing the various dimensions of burnout more frequently and more intensely than Maslach and Jackson's sample of human service workers. However, both on the emotional exhaustion and the depersonalization subscales, the average response of the officers was never as frequent as "a few times a month" and never as intense as "moderate." Furthermore, although the respondents reported lower levels of personal accomplishment than Maslach and Jackson's sample, they did report experiencing these feelings at least once a week and more than moderately. In other words, it appears that most officers were experiencing feelings of burnout on an infrequent and less than intense basis but that a sizable minority reported experiencing burnout both frequently and intensely. For example, as measured by the item about explicitly feeling "burned out," 13 percent of the respondents reported feeling this way "a few times a week" or "everyday," and another 7 percent reported feeling this way "once a week." Similarly, the item with the second highest loading on the factor of emotional exhaustion (pertaining to feeling emotionally drained) had a response pattern indicating that emotional exhaustion is an important problem for a sizable proportion of the workers. Specifically, 17 percent of the officers reported feeling drained either "a few times a week" or "everyday." Finally, to repeat a finding noted earlier concerning the personal accomplishment item about feeling that one is positively influencing other people's lives through one's work, 47 percent of the officers reported feeling this way only a few times a month at the most. In summary, on the one hand, it would be an exaggeration to paint an entirely negative picture; on the other hand, a sizable minority of the workers reported that they were experiencing negative feelings about their jobs.

SUMMARY

This chapter explained the sample, methodology, and descriptive findings concerning the probation/parole employees surveyed in July 1981. Perhaps the key methodological findings were that some intrinsic job satisfaction items loaded highly (about .40 or above) on Maslach and Jackson's personal accomplishment factor and that one factor solution suggested that personal accomplishment is actually two factors. Substantive findings showed that burnout is a problem for some, but not all, officers and that line officers in Connecticut were reporting the worst burnout scores in the sample.

Chapter 6 analyzes a path model of the burnout process in order to test key assumptions of the Maslach (1982) and Cherniss (1980a, 1980b) models of the sources of burnout.

NOTES

1. At the time of sample selection, a grant application was pending but not approved and the research was being planned on the assumption that it would be funded without the grant. Fortunately, a National Institute of Justice grant, which supported the research, was eventually approved.

2. Maslach Burnout Inventory-Human Services Survey by Christina Maslach & Susan E. Jackson, copyright 1981. Used with permission. The actual survey is available from the publisher, Consulting Psychologists Press Inc., Palo Alto, CA 94306.

Findings: Causes of Burnout 6

Lacking in much of the probation and parole literature has been an explicit causal modeling of the sources of the job problems that have been rather well described (see, again, Chapter 4 for a description of those job-related problems). This chapter attempts to fill that gap by presenting a causal model of job burnout in probation. Because the issue of job burnout is a complex one involving many variables at many levels of analysis (see Chapters 2 and 3), it would be extremely difficult to offer a complete causal model of the job burnout process. This chapter, however, represents an effort to test two of the leading theories of job burnout — those of Maslach (1982) and Cherniss (1980a, 1980b) — with data from probation officers.

METHODOLOGY

In addition to the issues raised in the methodology chapter (Chapter 5), several points should be noted. First, it was decided to focus on the New York State officers for this part of the research because the New York officers constituted the largest subgroup in the sample and because the New York sample offers an interesting set of contrasts. Specifically, the sample ranges from officers in large departments in large cities such as Buffalo and Rochester to officers in small, rural departments in isolated sections of the Adirondack region of the state. In this vein, even the weakness of the sample — the refusal of New York City to participate in the project — can be considered of positive value. Because New York City is so atypical by virtue of its size and attendant problems, any study of New York City risks being unrepresentative of other, smaller cities. More particularly, at the time of the study, New York City probation was not conducting home visits and was, therefore, unlike many other departments across the country. Although the chapter does focus on New York, reference will be made to the other subgroups (Indiana, Connecticut, and the Eastern District of Pennsylvania) where appropriate.

Second, path analysis is the technique (see, e.g., Asher, 1983) used to analyze the sources of burnout for the New York State officers. No claim is made that this technique proves causality in a definitive manner. Rather, path analysis represents an attempt to use survey data to examine possible sources of job burnout, especially in light of theoretical claims. Before any definitive causal claims are made, more research and different types of research are needed. For example, it seems appropriate to follow newly hired officers over time to see whether and how job burnout develops and what consequences occur. Likewise, it seems fitting to examine various interventions and then conduct follow-up research to determine if such interventions had any effect in preventing or reducing burnout.

A MODEL OF JOB BURNOUT FOR PROBATION OFFICERS

Figure 6.1 represents a model of the burnout process that allows for a test of the contrasting emphases of Maslach (1982) and Cherniss (1980a, 1980b), which were detailed in Chapters 2 and 3.

Proceeding from the more remote to the more immediate sources of burnout, both Maslach and Cherniss have noted that client (offender) contact is an important source of burnout. As previously noted, Maslach contends that contact with clients is the central cause of burnout: "For the professional helper overload translates into too many people and too little time to adequately serve their needs — a situation ripe for burnout" (Maslach, 1976, 1982; Pines & Maslach, 1980). Having too many clients is not the only problem, however; contact is also stressful because it centers on client problems, and thereby is emotionally charged, and because solutions for the problems are often difficult, if not impossible, to effect (Maslach & Jackson, 1981). In probation or parole work, for example, the offender may seek help only after he/she has committed a new crime and is facing the very real possibility of a (re)commitment to prison. Greater contact, therefore, was hypothesized to be positively correlated with more frequent feelings of burnout and role conflict (perception of overload) and negatively correlated with job satisfaction. Concerning the effect of contact on participation in decision making, Maslach (1982) has not specified a relationship. Cherniss (1980b) has implied that the stress of contact will lead line workers to turn to supervisors for assistance. Accordingly, it was hypothesized that contact and participation are positively correlated.

As noted in Chapter 2, Cherniss (1980b) has agreed that such client contact is a source of burnout, but he has differed from Maslach in indicating that client contact is only one part of the problem. The employing agency is the other part of the picture and very often the more important part. That is, Cherniss has agreed that client contact is stressful, but he has argued that the employing agency can do much to mitigate the problem. Supervisors, for example, can offer support to staff, including technical assistance, assistance in working through the feelings generated by the helping process, information, modeling, feedback, buffering against community groups or government agencies, advocacy for line staff vis-à-vis funding sources, and simple responsiveness. At the same time, supervisors must allow room for autonomy by being responsive to what workers want, that is, by allowing staff participation in decision making. Previous research has shown such participation in decision making to be correlated with less role conflict and greater job satisfaction (Cherniss, 1980b; Blumberg, 1976). This was the reason for incorporating participation in decision making into the model. It cannot reduce the objective workload

FIGURE 6.1 — A Model of the Job Burnout Process for Probation Officers

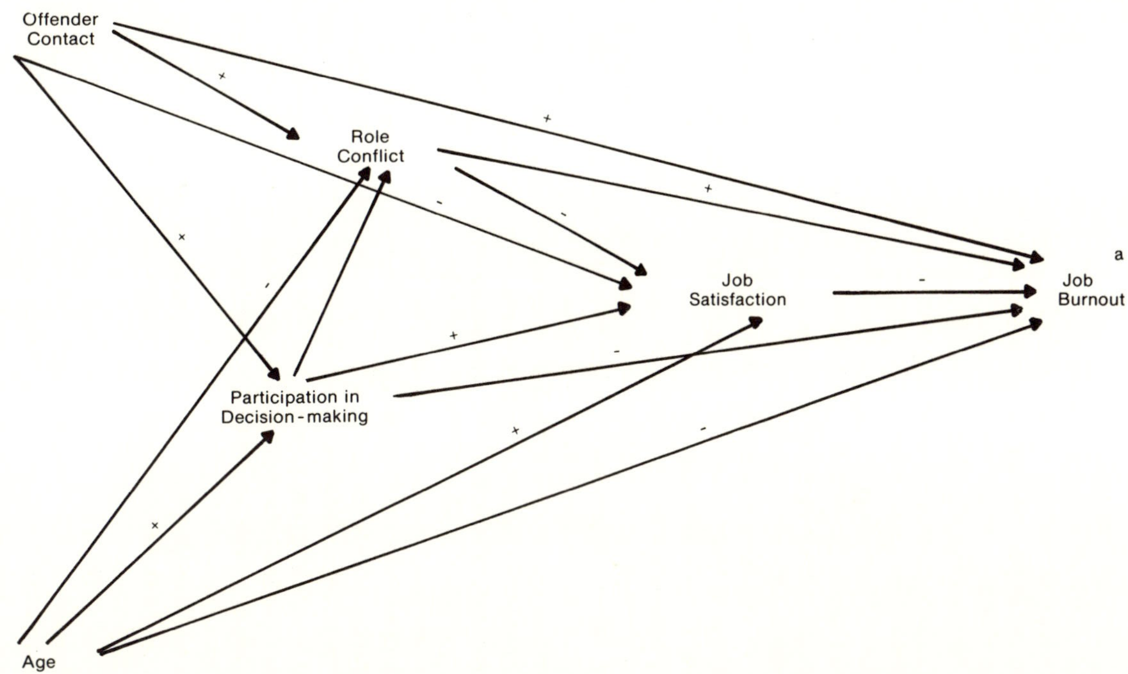

[a]Emotional Exhaustion, Depersonalization, and Personal Accomplishment.

(hours of offender contact), but it can reduce the perception of role conflict or excessive demands. If supervisors are responsive to line officers, the latter will not feel so overwhelmed. Maslach has not ignored supervisory responsiveness, but she has not emphasized it as much as Cherniss. In short, both theorists have claimed that participation in decision making mitigates the negative feelings of burnout; hence, participation should be negatively correlated with feelings of burnout.

Age was included in the model because both theorists included it in their accounts on both empirical and theoretical grounds. Maslach (1982) has found that younger workers usually score higher on burnout than older workers, a finding similar to that of lower job satisfaction among younger workers (Robinson, Athanasiou, & Head, 1978) and congruent with her interview data suggesting that younger workers who are unable to cope may leave human service work altogether (Maslach & Jackson, 1981). Furthermore, Maslach (1982, p. 59) has contended that age is not just an indicator of seniority: "'Older but wiser' seems to be the case here — with increased age, people are more stable and mature, have a more balanced perspective on life and are less prone to the excesses of burnout."

Cherniss has noted Maslach's findings on the relationship between age and burnout and also has noted that age may be important as an indicator of experience: "prior experience with the task, the stressor, and/or the situation attenuates the effects of stress" (Cherniss, 1980b, p. 136). Cherniss's point is that age can indicate past successful experience in stressful situations, which helps the worker to cope more effectively in similar situations in the future. The variable of seniority was examined in preliminary analyses, but it produced weaker relationships with the other study variables and thus was not included in the model. Given the positive association of age with reduced burnout and greater job satisfaction, it seems logical to expect similar relationships with role conflict and participation in decision making; that is, increasing age translates into less of a feeling of overload and more of a feeling of sharing. Furthermore, supervisors are more likely to consult older officers for opinions than younger, less mature, and less experienced officers. In short, age appears to reflect both greater maturity and past positive coping, and thus it was hypothesized to attenuate negative perceptions like exhaustion, depersonalization, and role conflict and to enhance positive attitudes such as job satisfaction and personal accomplishment.

Role conflict (perception of overload) was included in the model because it reflects the impact of objective overload on the individual and his/her ability to cope:

> Whether the coping involves a search for information, direct action, or even palliation, there will be an optimal length of time for the coping to occur. If there is not adequate time due to the constant intrusion of new demands, coping will be disrupted. The individual will tend to fall back on more primitive, less effective, more psychologically defensive coping behaviors (Cherniss, 1980b, p. 81).

Cherniss's point is that the objective workload may seem excessive on face value, but its subjective impact depends on the time available to handle the workload. Furthermore, Cherniss (1980b) has recognized the importance of individual capabilities and preferences, including the preference for challenge versus boredom. Maslach (1982) has noted the factor of individual ability to handle objective demands, but seems not to have emphasized it as much as Cherniss. Similarly, the inclusion of role conflict (perception of overload) as a variable follows the trend in current stress theory of conceptualizing stress as a person-environment fit problem (McMichael, 1978), in which objectively similar levels of demands may be perceived differently by various workers. In short, the inclusion of role conflict — the subjective evaluation of demands as excessive — was warranted by the literature. Role conflict was hypothesized to be positively correlated with exhaustion and depersonalization and negatively correlated with accomplishment and job satisfaction.

Job satisfaction was included because Maslach and Jackson (1981) (see Chapter 2) have claimed that job satisfaction is correlated only very weakly with burnout. Cherniss, however, has indicated that the correlation should be higher than Maslach and Jackson have indicated. Specifically, Cherniss (1980b, p. 16) has emphasized that "burnout is defined as psychological withdrawal from work in response to excessive stress or *dissatisfaction*" (emphasis added), which implies a higher correlation than the .20 level claimed by Maslach and Jackson (1981).

Finally, all three aspects of burnout — emotional exhaustion, depersonalization, and the personal accomplishment factor — were included as three distinct outcomes because this conceptualization follows the claim of Maslach and Jackson (1981) that these phenomena are distinct aspects of burnout. Maslach and Jackson (1980) originally indicated that exhaustion, depersonalization, and the absence of feelings of personal accomplishment are three sequential "phases" of the burnout process. This sequential conceptualization has been endorsed by Cherniss (1980b) and a more complex phasing has been postulated by Golembiewski, Munzenrider, and Stevenson (1986). For this research, however, each aspect of burnout was regressed separately on the logically prior variables, in accord with Maslach's current position.

In summary, Maslach's theory posits client contact as the central source of burnout whereas Cherniss's theory emphasizes both the individual's perception of overload (the role conflict variable in the model) and the organizational environment as more critical (hence, the inclusion of the participation variable). According to Cherniss, an organization responsive to the individual worker can override the negative impact of excessive demands. Also, Maslach has posited only a slight relationship between job satisfaction and burnout whereas Cherniss has included satisfaction as an important variable. The theorists have agreed, however, that age mitigates burnout because age represents both greater maturity and past, successful coping experiences.

FINDINGS

Table 6.1 includes the zero-order correlations, means, and standard deviations of the model variables. The largest zero-order correlates of emotional exhaustion and depersonalization were role conflict (the greater the perception of overload, the greater the burnout), job satisfaction (the lower the satisfaction, the greater the burnout), and age (decreasing burnout with increasing age). Participation in decision making was weakly correlated with exhaustion and personal accomplishment (those workers reporting greater participation also reported slightly less frequent feelings of exhaustion but more frequent feelings of accomplishment), and client contact correlated minimally with exhaustion and slightly with depersonalization. The largest zero-order correlates of personal accomplishment were job satisfaction — greater satisfaction was associated with more frequent feelings of accomplishment — and weekly hours of client contact. The more time spent in contact with probationers, the more frequent the feelings of accomplishment.

Table 6.2 shows the standardized path coefficients for the three aspects of burnout. Examination of the table shows that role conflict, job satisfaction, and age all had significant direct effects on emotional exhaustion: those officers who reported role conflict and lower satisfaction and those who were younger reported more frequent feelings of emotional exhaustion. Participation had no direct effect on exhaustion; hours of offender contact had no effect on exhaustion (contrary to Maslach's theory).

Role conflict, age, and job satisfaction, in decreasing order of importance, all had significant direct effects on depersonalization, and the effects were as predicted; those officers who were younger and reported role conflict and less satisfaction also reported more frequent feelings of depersonalization. Contrary to Maslach's theory, however, contact with probationers had no significant influence in generating an impersonal, cynical approach toward clients. Participation in decision making was not significantly related to depersonalization, but it was related significantly to both job satisfaction and role conflict.

Only job satisfaction and weekly hours of client contact had any significant direct effects on personal accomplishment; contrary to Maslach, job satisfaction and accomplishment varied directly and considerably (.56), and, also contrary to Maslach, greater client contact was associated with more frequent feelings of accomplishment, rather than being a stressor causing a less frequent sense of accomplishment.

Table 6.3 presents a decomposition of the effects of each variable into direct, indirect, total, and noncausal effects (see Nie et al., 1975, for an explanation; see also Asher, 1983). Role conflict exercised almost all of its effect directly on exhaustion and depersonalization, but the effect of role conflict on accomplishment was largely indirect through the satisfaction variable. Almost all the effect of satisfaction on accomplishment was direct whereas much of the effect of satisfaction on exhaustion was not. Offender contact had no significant indirect effects on the model variables. Finally, both age and participation exercised much of their effects through other variables.

TABLE 6.1
Intercorrelations, Means, and Standard Deviations of the Model Variables

Variable	2	3	4	5	6	7	8	*M*[a]	*SD*
(1) Age	.00	-.04	-.13	.14	-.23	-.25	.13	35.1	9.6
(2) Weekly hours of offender contact	--	.05	-.06	.11	-.03	-.11	.24	17.3	6.5
(3) Participation in decision-making		--	-.22	.35	-.17	-.03	.17	2.87	0.87
(4) Role conflict (perceived overload)			.--	-.31	.46	.30	-.19	3.37	0.66
(5) Job satisfaction				--	-.34	-.24	.58	4.13	1.10
(6) Emotional exhaustion					--	.51	-.24	2.31	1.11
(7) Depersonalization						--	-.36	1.72	1.14
(8) Personal accomplishment							--	4.14	0.88

[a]Due to item phrasing, higher scores reflect more frequent emotional exhaustion, depersonalization, and personal accomplishment, greater job satisfaction, greater role conflict, greater participation, and more hours of offender contact.

$n = 387$; listwise deletion.

TABLE 6.2
Standardized Path Coefficients and Adjusted R^2s for the Job Burnout Model

	2	3	4	5	Emotional Exhaustion	Depersonal-ization	Personal Accomplishment
(1) Age	.00	-.04	-.14*	.12*	-.15*	-.19*	.05
(2) Weekly hours of offender contact		.05	-.05	.08	.02	-.08	.18*
(3) Participation in decision-making			-.22*	.30*	-.02	.07	-.03
(4) Role conflict				-.23*	.38*	.24*	-.00
(5) Job satisfaction					-.20*	-.16*	.56*
Adjusted R^2	.00	.00	.06*	.19*	.27*	.15*	.36*

Note: When nonsignificant paths were deleted and the model reestimated, only minimal alterations occurred in the parameter estimates, and there were no changes in the significant paths.
$p < .05$

TABLE 6.3
Decomposition Table: Summary of Effects in Path Models of Burnout

	Correlation	Direct	Indirect	Total	Non-causal
EMOTIONAL EXHAUSTION					
Age	-.23	-.15	-.08	-.23	.00
Offender contact	-.03	.02	-.04	-.02	-.01
Participation in decision-making	-.17	-.02	-.15	-.17	.00
Role conflict	.46	.38	.05	.43	.03
Job satisfaction	-.34	-.20	--	-.20	-.14
DEPERSONALIZATION					
Age	-.25	-.19	-.06	-.25	.00
Offender contact	-.11	-.08	-.02	-.10	-.01
Participation in decision-making	-.03	.07	-.10	-.03	.00
Role conflict	.30	.24	.04	.28	.02
Job satisfaction	-.24	-.16	--	-.16	-.08
PERSONAL ACCOMPLISHMENT					
Age	.13	.05	.07	.12	.01
Offender contact	.24	.18	.04	.22	.02
Participation in decision-making	.17	-.03	.17	.14	.03
Role conflict	-.19	-.00	-.13	-.13	-.06
Job satisfaction	.58	.56	--	.56	.02

Note: For an explanation of decomposition, see Nie et al. (1975, pp. 388–89).

The three path models of the three aspects of burnout were also run with caseload (monthly numbers of adult and juvenile supervision cases) included as a variable. Caseload was not related significantly to either depersonalization or personal accomplishment; however, it did have a significant effect on exhaustion (path coefficient about –.10; that is, the higher the caseload, the lower the exhaustion). As with offender contact, the other model variables were more important.

Findings for Connecticut and Indiana

The burnout measures were also analyzed for the line officers in Connecticut and Indiana to see if there were any significant variations by state in the models. This allows some examination of the possibility that burnout varies with organizational setting, given the differences in the organization of probation in the three states noted in Chapter 5.

The findings in Connecticut showed only one major variation. Job satisfaction was related only to the accomplishment dimension of burnout; satisfaction did not show a statistically significant relationship to either exhaustion or depersonalization. Because only about 70 line officers participated in the Connecticut sample, however, these results must be interpreted with caution.

The findings in Indiana were more interesting. Weekly hours of contact with probationers showed a significant relationship with emotional exhaustion (correlation = .26; standardized regression coefficient = .17). Furthermore, contact was not related to either depersonalization or personal accomplishment. Also, role conflict had no significant effect on either depersonalization or accomplishment for the Indiana probation officers.

Addendum: Variables Not Included in the Path Analysis

Several variables not included in the path analysis deserve further attention, especially because they will be discussed further in the implications section of Chapter 11.

As noted, age was included instead of seniority. Separate analyses of the burnout scores and seniority, however, indicated that the relationship between seniority and burnout was curvilinear. In other words, new workers with less than six months of experience reported the least frequent feelings of burnout, and more experienced workers reported more frequent feelings of burnout. Workers with 15 years or more of experience, however, reported the lowest depersonalization scores and the second lowest emotional exhaustion scores.

Measures of exercise, marital status, religiosity, number of children in one's care, and support were not included in the path analysis because separate analyses indicated that these variables were not significantly related to the burnout measures. As will be noted in Chapter 11, however, because these variables did not increase burnout, perhaps the best conclusion about the importance of these variables is that further research is needed.

Perhaps the measures used in this particular study were not adequate to uncover the relationships that the review of the burnout and probation/parole literatures suggested would exist between these variables and burnout.

DISCUSSION AND IMPLICATIONS

The most dramatic finding of this analysis was a negative one. In both New York State and Connecticut, contact with probationers had no significant effect on emotional exhaustion or depersonalization, and in New York the effect on accomplishment was diametrically opposed to burnout theory — greater contact was associated with more frequent feelings of accomplishment. Furthermore, offender contact also had no significant effect on the (New York) model variables — job satisfaction, role conflict, and participation in decision making. Quite simply, Maslach's theory of the burnout process, emphasizing client contact as a chronic stressor leading to burnout, was not accurate for these two samples of probation officers. Indiana, however, did show the predicted relationship between client contact and the emotional exhaustion dimension of burnout, but contact had no relationship with the other two aspects of burnout.

There are at least two possible explanations for the failure of Maslach's theory to account for probation officer burnout (except for the isolated corroborative finding from Indiana). One explanation is that her theory is appropriate for most human service occupations but not for probation, because the nature of client contact is radically different in probation or parole work. Unlike most human service fields, in which clients seek out workers and burden them with emotionally laden problems (McCleary, 1978), it appears that past descriptions of client contact in probation/parole were accurate when they assessed the contact between offender and officer in community supervision as "typically, amiable, superficial, and brief" (Stanley, 1976, p. 97). Such superficial supervision has been explained as stemming from high caseloads (Stanley, 1976), parolee desires to avoid officer surveillance (Irwin, 1970), officer laziness and involvement in non-job-related pursuits (McCleary, 1978), and the lack of service technology (i.e., lack of resources to provide practical assistance to parolees) (Studt, 1973). Although the present research had no measure of the quality of officer-offender contacts, the findings on the quantity of contact — respondents reported only about 17 hours per week in direct contact with probationers — suggest that the quality was not intense. Seventeen hours per week, even if it is not an overly generous estimate of actual client contact, hardly seems the onus that Maslach has described in her analysis of burnout. Probation and parole officers apparently spend most of their time doing things other than people-work, and yet Maslach has claimed that people-work is a critical condition for burnout. Client contact may have to reach a certain critical mass, arguably more than 17 hours per week, before burnout will be a problem. Such an explanation is congruent with the present findings on the relative lack of importance of client contact as a source of burnout and the relatively low levels of burnout per se in the sample (on the average, officers reported feelings of emotional exhaustion or depersonalization only about once a month or less).

The second possible explanation for the lack of importance of client contact as a causal variable in the burnout process is that Maslach's model is too simplistic, whereas Cherniss's model is both more detailed and more accurate. Several findings support such an interpretation. First, Cherniss has placed more emphasis than Maslach both on the individual worker's assessment of the level of demands placed on him or her and on the employing agency as a critical factor. Cherniss has pointed out, for example, that organizational policies or practices can effectively mitigate the negative impact of such objective sources of burnout as excessive contact with clients. Second, the importance of role conflict in the analysis indicates that the officer's perception of overload or excessive demands is much more important than the simple amount of offender contact inherent in the job; this is congruent with Cherniss (1980b) and with current stress theory, which emphasizes the person-environment fit model of the stress process (see, e.g., McMichael, 1978). The significant influence of participation in decision making on job satisfaction and role conflict also is consistent with Cherniss — organizational responsiveness to workers can be beneficial. Finally, Cherniss has accorded job satisfaction a more important role in the burnout process than has Maslach; some support for this position is provided in the present analysis, especially the substantial effect of job satisfaction on the personal accomplishment aspect of burnout. Clearly, high job satisfaction is associated with less frequent feelings of exhaustion and depersonalization and more frequent feelings of accomplishment.

Whatever the correct interpretation of the finding of the lack of importance of offender contact as a source of burnout may be, the clear implication is that reducing the amount of contact will not, in and of itself, prevent or reduce burnout for probation officers. In fact, some of the responses of the officers indicate that many enjoy offender contact; 51 percent reported that they frequently have a positive impact on offenders' lives, and about a third reported that they frequently feel exhilarated after contact with offenders. Because officers arguably do not enjoy a sense of being overloaded or having high caseloads, the implication for managers is to find ways for officers to maintain direct interaction with offenders, regardless of all the other demands on their time. This is consistent with the research of Thomson and Fogel (1980), which found paperwork to be the major problem confronting probation officers and lack of community resources the second most important problem, with no mention of any stress from client contact.

A cautionary implication of the findings on the lack of influence of client contact on burnout and on the low levels of burnout in the sample is that these findings do not imply that all is well with probation and parole officers. The finding from Indiana suggests that client contact may be problematic. Furthermore, as noted in Chapter 1, Clear (1985, p. 40), for example, has described probation as "an early-career position which most people leave to take other jobs," a situation that he has attributed to a set of disincentives such as problems with promotions and pay increments, such that "good performance remains virtually unrewarded, and the greatest available reward — promotion — is sometimes given to those whose work is perceived by colleagues as wanting in quality" (Clear, 1985, p. 41). Although it was not reported here (but will be noted later for the entire sample [see Chapter 8]), the officers in New York State echoed such concerns. Eighty-eight percent were dissatisfied with promotional opportunities, and 71 percent were dissatisfied with the pay. Clear's (1985) suggestions for change in this area are the implementation of performance-based evaluations and rewards and the creation of a career ladder in which line officers would not have to abandon supervision of offenders for supervision of staff, rather than continuation of the current, problem-ridden civil service or patronage reward systems.

The importance of job satisfaction as a correlate of burnout may appear initially to be one more instance of social science demonstrating the obvious; however, Maslach, a pioneer in burnout research, specifically disclaimed any strong correlation between the two variables (Maslach & Jackson, 1981). At least for probation employees, her contention is simply not accurate. The importance of job satisfaction in the analysis suggests that whatever improves job satisfaction will reduce burnout. Unlike the research on burnout, which is relatively recent, the research on job satisfaction has been going on for more than 50 years; one recent review counted 3,300 previous studies of the matter (Locke, 1976). The satisfaction research, moreover, has been showing a consistent pattern; the research clearly has been answering the question of how jobs can be designed to satisfy and motivate workers:

> Both common sense and research answer these questions in terms of variety, complexity, autonomy, and responsibility. . . . Studies show negative relations . . . between external control of work pace and satisfaction. In fact, the bulk of the research on satisfaction with jobs demonstrates that more varied, complex and challenging tasks are higher in worker gratification than less skilled routine jobs (Katz & Kahn, 1978, p. 364).

Managers, therefore, can utilize the plethora of job satisfaction information in the fight against burnout, confident that interventions suggested by such research will have some effect on burnout.

The findings also suggest that probation managers should pay special attention to younger, less senior workers. Specifically, the path analysis showed an inverse relationship between age and burnout; younger workers reported more frequent burnout than older workers. Two interventions seem possible. First, it is critical to initiate an effective orientation program, if one is not already in place, or to improve the existing program, if scrutiny indicates that it needs improvement. Such an orientation program need not be elaborate and expensive to be effective. Even a realistic orientation booklet or one- or two-day programs can be effective, if they present problems likely to occur and some proven methods of coping (Cherniss, 1980b), rather than merely detailing organization fringe benefits. An effective orientation program or booklet may minimize the reality shock (Kramer, 1974) that many young, idealistic workers, especially recent graduates, face as they enter correctional employment. If nothing is done for the younger workers, no doubt some of the "'good people' who are frequently in such short supply" (Martinson, 1974, p. 46) may leave the field, and probation will continue to be the early-career position that Clear (1985) described it to be. The second possible intervention is a mentoring program (Cherniss, 1980b) in which experienced officers could orient newly hired officers during the initial period of employment and thereby share their coping skills with new officers. Care would be needed to select mentors who would not socialize new officers into organizational deviance (see McCleary, 1978, for an example of this), but would share positive attitudes.

Finally, the results suggest the need for further research. Participation in decision making, for example, mitigated role conflict and enhanced job satisfaction but had no direct effects on burnout; perhaps a better measure of participation would show more impact. Perhaps these findings are limited to New York State (and, where applicable, to Connecticut and Indiana); research in other locations may lead to different results. What has been shown, however, is that, at least for officers in a large, northeastern state, the rather simplistic Maslach model of job burnout is not as appropriate as Cherniss's more complex model.

SUMMARY

This chapter has presented a path analytic test of many of the key propositions of the burnout theories of Maslach (1982) and Cherniss (1980a, 1980b). The findings indicated that client contact was not a significant source of burnout for probation officers in New York State but that organizational problems such as role conflict were related to burnout scores. Thus, the data showed greater support for Cherniss's more comprehensive model of the burnout process.

The analysis also showed that both job satisfaction and age were significantly related to burnout. Thus, managers should focus attention on younger workers and can derive intervention suggestions from the job satisfaction literature.

The next chapter devotes specific attention to gender differences in burnout. Given the increased emphasis in criminology and criminal justice on women offenders, women victims, and women practitioners, it is appropriate to analyze the job experiences of women officers. This is especially appropriate given the large number of women probation and parole officers compared to the relatively small number of women in policing.

Gender and Burnout 7

In the last 15 years, considerable attention has been devoted to the topic of women in criminal justice. Some writers have focused on the issue of female involvement in crime (e.g., Adler, 1975; Simon, 1975; Weisheit, 1984; Wilson, 1981; Wolfe, Cullen, & Cullen, 1984), including the adequacy of criminological theory to explain female criminality (Leonard, 1982). Other researchers have directed attention to women in policing (Martin, 1980; Remington, 1981; Townsey, 1982; Wexler & Logan, 1983), and still others have examined the topic of females in prison, both as prisoners and as correctional officers (Crouch & Alpert, 1982; Etheridge, Hale, & Hambrick, 1984; Mahan, 1984; Owen, 1985; Price & Sokoloff, 1982; Zimmer, 1986). Entire courses are now devoted to female criminality and to women in the criminal justice system.

Surprisingly, interest in women probation and parole officers has been almost nonexistent amid all the interest in female offenders and law enforcement officers. Recent books on women in the criminal justice system (Flowers, 1987; Price & Sokoloff, 1982), for example, included articles on women judges, lawyers, police, and correctional officers, but none on probation or parole officers. Even basic information on the extent of female employment in probation and parole, both currently and trends over time, has not been as readily available as the same information on women in policing. What is so surprising about this wholesale lack of attention is that women — as far as can be seen from the incomplete information available — constitute a substantial proportion of those employed in community supervision (American Correctional Association, 1981) and may be better parole officers than males (Waller, 1974).

This chapter focuses on women as officers. Specifically, the analysis centers on whether women officers are different from their male counterparts in job burnout and job dissatisfaction and in possible sources of such job distress, including work load differentials and differences in the work setting (such as role conflict).

This focus on women officers is important regardless of the results. Any differences would suggest that there is a need to address the specific needs and concerns of female officers. A lack of differences would indicate that the problems in probation and parole employment are transsexual — they apply to both genders equally — and it would be diversionary to focus on gender as an explanatory variable. If the latter is the case, then the lack of attention given to women in the past was perhaps regrettable but not consequential. Finally, this chapter is significant because it allows an examination of a criminal justice work environment, probation, where women constitute a substantial proportion of the employee population, in contrast to both policing and prison, where women officers are far less represented.

BACKGROUND

Chapter 4 showed that considerable attention has been devoted to the work problems of probation and parole officers. The overwhelming majority of studies on probation and parole, however, have not directed any attention to gender differences between male and female officers.

Two exceptions to this widespread neglect of female officers were written over a decade ago (Schoonmaker & Brooks, 1975; Stout, 1973). Both considered the generic issue of the employment of female officers and the specific issue of officers, female or male, supervising offenders of the opposite sex.

One recent exception to this pattern offers a suggestion for the previous neglect. Golden (1982) examined the interests of female college students concerning employment in policing, probation, and other criminal justice occupations and found that role-innovative occupations (e.g., police) were not as attractive to women criminal justice students as were traditional, female-role-compatible specialties (e.g., probation). This implies that the role of probation officer, like that of social worker, teacher, or nurse, represents a role quite consistent with traditional conceptions of women. The lack of research on women in probation may stem, therefore, from a view of the entire field as being more appropriate for females than for males; hence, the issue of female officers may have been considered either uninteresting or the norm. Women police officers received research scrutiny because of the intriguing incongruity between traditional stereotypes of women and the police officer role.

Other references to women in probation or parole are less clearcut. Norland and Mann (1984), for example, noted that male officers reported feeling uncomfortable and incompetent in dealing with the interpersonal problems of female probationers, but these authors never noted that perhaps the simple solution would be to hire more female officers. Frazier, Bock, and Henretta (1983) looked at the issue of whether offenders receive different sentence recommendations in presentence reports because of gender and found that the gender of the officer did not matter; male and female officers alike emphasized previous record and severity for male criminals but focused on emotional stability and family relationships for female offenders. Potts (1983) reviewed the equal employment issue for women in corrections but gave only one paragraph to one case dealing with alleged discrimination of women probation officers seeking promotion, as compared to pages devoted to a number of cases concerning discrimination toward female correctional officers. More as a parenthetical remark than a substantive finding, Waller (1974, pp. 210–11) observed that the "sex of the workers seems not to be an entirely irrelevant fact. Parolees often felt that they were more at ease with, and got more help from, an older, perhaps middle-aged woman." The most recent mention of gender as an issue concerning probation officers was Walsh's (1984) finding that female officers defined sexual assault as less serious than did male officers and consequently offered significantly more lenient sentences for such sex offenders than did male officers.

The burnout literature offers contrasting suggestions about the importance of gender in relation to burnout. Maslach (1982, p. 58) observed, "Overall, men and women are fairly similar in their experience of burnout," and Cherniss (1980b) did not even mention gender as a possible individual factor in the causation of burnout. Maslach found statistically significant differences in the burnout levels reported by her subjects: "Women tend to experience more emotional exhaustion, and to experience it more intensely than men. However, men are more likely to have depersonalized and callous feelings about the people they work with" (1982, p. 52). Maslach related these differences in burnout levels to differences in the socialization process:

> Women are expected to be more oriented toward people than are men — they are supposed to be nurturant, sociable, and sensitive to people's feelings. They are also supposed to be very emotional people themselves, while men are supposed to be hard, tough, and unemotional (The "big boys don't cry" stereotype) (1982, p. 58).

In other words, women are more likely to weary of the nurturant demands placed on them but are less likely than men to let people-work burdens harden them into either an impersonal or a cynical approach.

Although Cherniss (1980a, 1980b) failed to consider gender as an important variable in relation to burnout, his model of the burnout process (see Chapter 3) does not preclude gender differences. Because his model emphasizes job and organizational sources of burnout, any systematic sex differentials in such matters as autonomy, participation in decision making, or role conflict could clearly result in differential outcomes. For example, it could be the case that male administrators systematically limit promotional opportunities and/or substantial pay increments for women officers, but not for males. Hence, administrative practices might be sources of burnout for female officers.

More recently, Etzion and Pines (1986) found that U.S. and Israeli women reported higher burnout (exhaustion scores) than men. Cultural differences, however, were larger than gender differences.

In summary, the leading burnout theoreticians favor the hypothesis that gender is not an important correlate of job burnout, although they do provide for gender differences. The probation/parole literature is equivocal concerning the question of whether gender makes any difference in the job attitudes and perceptions of officers. On the one hand, officers did not differ in their presentence report recommendations; on the other hand, women college students were rather traditional in their career aspirations in criminal justice, and women who interviewed parolees were better able to establish rapport with parolees than were male parole officers. Thus, at least some of the research on probation/parole suggests that women officers are more people oriented and nurturant than are male officers and, as Maslach suggests, might very well tire of the job demands but still be less likely to treat their clients in a depersonalized manner.

METHODOLOGY

It was decided to focus on the line officers in the sample for the examination of the effects of gender. Analysis of variance and multiple regression techniques were used to examine differences in burnout scores.

FINDINGS

Table 7.1 presents the mean scores and oneway analysis of variance findings on the three factors of job burnout for both female and male officers. Three points stand out. First, only two of the six burnout scores showed significant differences for male and female officers. Second, the significant differences (and the differences that approached statistical significance) were as predicted by Maslach; that is, females scored or tended to score higher on emotional exhaustion and lower on depersonalization. Third, the statistically significant differences were hardly substantively significant; fractional differences on a seven-point measure hardly seem the basis for sweeping policy changes.

TABLE 7.1
Oneway Analyses of Variance for Burnout, Job Satisfaction, and Role Conflict Measures by Gender

	Male officers		Female officers		F
Variables	M	SD	M	SD	
Emotional exhaustion (f)	2.30	1.17	2.47	1.10	3.56
Emotional exhaustion (i)	3.54	1.40	3.80	1.33	6.00*
Depersonalization (f)	1.86	1.23	1.73	1.13	1.86
Depersonalization (i)	2.88	1.57	2.63	1.53	4.22*
Personal accomplishment (f)	4.12	0.92	4.08	0.87	0.31
Personal accomplishment (i)	4.80	0.89	4.85	0.79	0.50
Intrinsic job satisfaction (f)	4.03	1.03	4.05	0.94	0.09
Intrinsic job satisfaction (i)	4.66	0.98	4.71	0.86	0.36
Role conflict	2.59	0.71	2.65	0.71	1.40

Note: (f) = frequency dimension; (i) = intensity dimension.
n varied from 678 to 706; pairwise deletion used.
*$p < .05$.

Table 7.1 also shows that the intrinsic job satisfaction and role conflict scores were not significantly different for males and females.

Similarly, Table 7.2 shows that there were no significant gender differences in probation work load, as measured by the variables of total number of hours worked per week, number of hours spent in client contact per week, and number of investigations conducted per month. Caseload differences were significant, but caseload has been criticized for being a vague and inaccurate measure of actual work load. For example, officers with high caseloads may use caseload as an excuse for not doing work, and such officers may actually expend less effort than do officers with much smaller caseloads (see, e.g., McCleary, 1978).

Given such a lack of differences between men and women, the chapter could end here with a discussion of the reasons for such similarity. Before proceeding to that discussion, however, it seems necessary to consider the possibility that an examination of differences in mean scores between male and female officers is just too simplistic. Perhaps controlling for marital status or children would show gender differences. The argument here is that females are differentially affected by family responsibilities vis-à-vis males (see, e.g., Cleary & Mechanic, 1983; Gore & Mangione, 1983; Haw, 1982, for a discussion of these issues); many claim that women still shoulder most of the childrearing and housekeeping duties in addition to job-related responsibilities.

To examine this possibility, the emotional exhaustion, depersonalization, and personal accomplishment scores were regressed on sex, marital status, number of children, caseload size, weekly hours of client contact, role conflict, age, and job satisfaction. As Table 7.3 shows, gender was not a significant predictor of either the emotional exhaustion or the personal accomplishment aspect of burnout, but gender was a significant

TABLE 7.2
Oneway Analyses of Variance for Measures of Work Load by Gender

	Male officers		Female officers		F
Variables	M	SD	M	SD	
Hours worked per week	38.0	4.95	38.5	5.73	1.63
Hours of offender contact per week	16.3	6.28	17.1	7.25	2.69
Investigations per month	6.3	6.82	6.6	6.67	0.36
Adult caseload	48.2	52.84	36.9	53.77	7.55*
Juvenile caseload	8.5	17.42	12.8	19.16	9.20*

Note: n varied from 678 to 706; pairwise deletion used.
$^*p < .05$.

TABLE 7.3
Regression Results of Burnout Measures on Selected Variables, Including Gender

Independent Variables	Emotional Exhaustion Beta	Emotional Exhaustion t-value	Depersonalization Beta	Depersonalization t-value	Personal Accomplishment Beta	Personal Accomplishment t-value
Gender[a]	.04	1.13	-.10*	-2.56	-.03	-0.97
Caseload[b]	.02	0.62	.13*	3.54	-.04	-1.34
Age	-.15*	-4.02	-.18*	-4.66	.02	0.67
Weekly hours of offender contact	.07*	2.03	-.05	-1.42	.16*	4.99
Job satisfaction	-.22*	-6.18	-.18*	-4.78	.57*	17.05
Role Conflict	-.38*	-10.62	-.21*	-5.35	-.00	-0.06
Marital Status[c]	.04	0.99	.04	0.97	-.01	-0.31
Children[d]	-.03	-.074	-.05	-1.23	-.02	-0.65
R^2	.29*		.18*		.37*	

Note: $n = 624$; listwise deletion used.
*$p < .05$.
[a]Gender: female = 1; male = 0.
[b]Caseload size is the aggregate of adult and juvenile supervision cases, investigations, and intakes handled by the officer in a typical month.
[c]Coded dichotomously: married = 1; not married = 0.
[d]Coded dichotomously: 1 or more children = 1; no children = 0.

predictor of depersonalization. Job satisfaction, role conflict, and age were far more important correlates of the aspects of burnout than was gender.

DISCUSSION

Contrary to some of the emphasis concerning possible gender differences in criminal behavior or to the expectations concerning the introduction of women police officers (Remington, 1981), the findings here revealed little or no difference between male and female probation officers. Most of the differences were not statistically significant; those few that were significant were not of sufficient magnitude to generate concern. The significant differences in the burnout scores, for example, were only about .25 on a seven-point scale — not a basis for recommending differential research or policy attention to female officers.

These null findings are consistent with the previously mentioned claim of Maslach (1982, p. 58) that "[O]verall, men and women are fairly similar in their experience of burnout." They are also consistent with previous research on police, which found no attitudinal differences between male and female officers on measures of organizational commitment, job satisfaction, role conflict, and role ambiguity (Fry & Greenfeld, 1980) and with the research of Frazier, Bock, and Henretta (1983), which found no officer gender differences in presentence report recommendations.

Given such an absence of differences, the logical question is why the differences were nonexistent or miniscule. The best answer seems to be that male and female officers did not differ on the hypothesized causes of burnout. Men and women reported approximately similar work loads, approximately similar levels of job satisfaction and satisfaction with pay and promotional opportunities, and approximately similar degrees of role conflict. Thus, both men and women reported similar levels of burnout (an outcome measure) because they were facing essentially similar levels of the sources of burnout. In other words, their task environments and organizational environments were quite similar.

Another answer may be that the presence of women in substantial numbers in the work environment, together with the nature of the work — people-work but with elements of control and authority over clients — has created an androgynous environment that combines important elements of the "masculine" and "feminine" roles. Other criminal justice work environments may well profit from such an atmosphere.

The clearest implication of this finding of little or no difference is that specific attention to the needs of women officers is not important either for researchers or for policy makers. Apparently, the problems of women officers are the problems of male officers, so neither gender requires special attention.

One caveat to this is the possibility that the findings of no difference stem from the self-selection of the males who enter probation employment. That is, perhaps the males who become officers resemble females in personality more closely than they resemble males who choose careers in law enforcement, institutional corrections, sales management, or other traditionally "masculine" occupations. Arguably, probation, much like teaching or nursing, may be a field that attracts individuals, male or female, who are more nurturant and people oriented and less concerned with profit, authority, and control. Thus, gender may not be exercising any influence on job burnout because the personality differences traditionally and stereotypically associated with gender may not be present in this "feminine" occupation.

This research did not measure personality, and thus there is no empirical way to test this line of reasoning in this sample. However, some indirect support for the argument exists in that 50 percent of the 711 male and female officers reported previous experience in social work or people-work occupations, whereas only 5 percent reported previous law enforcement experience. An argument to the contrary, however, is that past research has indicated that male officers are far from nurturant. Specifically, Norland

and Mann (1984) found that male probation officers considered female probationers troublesome because they presented atypical problems, interpersonal or emotional difficulties that were beyond the competence of male officers. Given such a negative view of female probationers, it would be difficult to argue that male probation officers are nurturant or feminine.

Another self-selection explanation is that perhaps the females entering probation employment are more masculine than females in general and thus would be more likely to report the same burnout scores as male officers. This argument is purely speculative; the research here offers no support for it, and Golden's (1982) research on female student career choices does not support such a contention, as the students opted for traditional, role-compatible specialties.

Apart from the reasons for the lack of differences, the findings suggest that those who do the hiring in probation need not fear that women are more likely than men to burn out and then quit, or to cope by treating probationers in a depersonalized manner. Clearly there are no such grounds for not hiring either females or males; each gender is equally likely to experience the problem of job burnout.

Concerning future research, it would be diversionary to call for the administration of personality inventories to officer candidates. Although such research could determine if the males entering probation employment are indeed exhibiting personality traits traditionally associated with females or with occupations usually viewed as more feminine than masculine, the findings in this report indicate that whatever differences exist, they do not matter in an environment such as probation, where there are substantial numbers of female employees. The question for future research in probation settings, therefore, is not whether women or men are more prone to job problems such as burnout, but whether officers, regardless of gender, can avoid such problems and how the organization can assist all employees in that goal. The question for other criminal justice agencies where women are not so well represented is whether increasing the number of female employees might decrease some of the problems that women experience on the job, especially the lack of acceptance by male employees (e.g., Remington, 1981; Wexler & Logan, 1983; Zimmer, 1986).

Managers and Burnout 8

Managerial personnel in probation have been like a popular comedian who "doesn't get no respect." In other words, the research literature (see Chapter 4) has usually neglected managers in any consideration of the job-related problems in the field (see, e.g., Polisky, 1981a, 1981b; Studt, 1973; Waller, 1974). Attention to managerial personnel, however, is warranted for several reasons. First, the stress literature (e.g., Burke & Weir, 1980) and the burnout literature (e.g., Vash, 1980) indicate that managers in human service agencies also experience job-related difficulties that can lead to burnout. Second, probation administrators are responsible for policy formulation (Smykla, 1984) and direct supervisors are critical interpreters and modifiers of policy at the street level (McCleary, 1978). Third, in addition to these task-related aspects of organizational life, managers also serve as sources of socioemotional support for line officers, and such support is critical both for organizational effectiveness (Katz & Kahn, 1978) and the prevention or reduction of line officer job burnout (Cherniss, 1980b; Shapiro, 1982). Fourth, in many agencies, especially smaller ones, these employees also may function as line officers who supervise caseloads, conduct investigations, and perform intake screenings; these human contact tasks are considered critical factors in the etiology of burnout (Maslach, 1976, 1982). In fact, where they function as line officers, managers may be especially susceptible to burnout because they may be even more overloaded than line officers without administrative responsibilities. In short, although probation managerial personnel are critical agents in the organization, their experiences and attitudes have not been adequately addressed.

METHODS

This chapter focuses on the responses of probation directors, chief probation officers, assistant directors or chiefs, and supervisors (managerial N = 183). Mean scores, frequencies, and oneway analysis of variance were used for the comparisons in this chapter.

FINDINGS

Demographic Findings

The managers were mostly male, white, married college graduates. Specifically, 75 percent were male, 95 percent were Caucasian, 72 percent were married, and only 9 percent had less than a baccalaureate degree. Conversely, 25 percent were women, 4 percent were minority members, 15 percent were single, 12 percent were separated or divorced, and 34 percent had some type of master's degree. The average age of the managers was 41.7 years and the median was 39.3; the youngest was 22, and the oldest, 66 years of age. Seniority in probation work varied from almost none to more than 15 years; 54 percent reported between 5 and 15 years of experience, and 35 percent reported 15 years or more of experience.

Forty-four percent (N = 81) of the managers were supervisors with direct responsibility over line officers; 56 percent (N = 102) were upper-level administrators, including probation directors, deputy directors, chief probation officers, or assistant chiefs. In the rest of the chapter, the upper-level administrators will be termed administrators and the lower-level supervisors will be termed supervisors.

Fifty-eight percent (N = 106) of the respondents were from New York State, 31 percent (N = 57) were from Indiana, 8 percent (N = 6) were from Connecticut, and 3.3 percent (N = 6) were from the Eastern District of Pennsylvania (i.e., federal workers in Philadelphia or Reading). Seventy-five percent (N = 137) reported that they worked between 35 and 40 hours a week; 42 percent (N = 76) reported no client contact in a typical week, but 28 percent (N = 51) reported ten or more hours of contact with probationers in a typical week.

Substantive Findings

Table 8.1 presents the mean burnout scores for all managerial personnel and for upper management (administrators) compared to front-line supervisors (supervisors). Examination of the table shows that burnout was not a pervasive problem for the probation managerial personnel in the sample. On the average, managerial personnel reported experiencing

TABLE 8.1
Mean Burnout Scores for Probation Managers

	Emotional Exhaustion			Depersonalization			Personal Accomplishment		
	All	Adms.	Sups.	All	Adms.	Sups.	All	Adms.	Sups.
M	2.08	1.99	2.20	1.58	1.43	1.82	4.06	4.11	3.97
SD	1.27	1.23	1.33	1.20	1.14	1.28	1.02	0.98	1.10
Cases	166	94	72	110	69	41	102	65	37

Note: "All" = all managerial personnel; "Adms." = upper management; "Sups." = line supervisors.

None of the differences between administrators and supervisors were significant at the .05 level, but the depersonalization scores were different at the .10 level (analysis of variance).

feelings of emotional exhaustion about once a month, feelings of depersonalization less frequently than once a month, and feelings of personal accomplishment about once a week. There were no significant differences between administrators and supervisors at the .05 level, although the differences on the depersonalization scale approached that level of significance (actual significance = .095).

Table 8.2 clarifies the extent of burnout in the sample by presenting managerial responses to specific items from the Maslach Burnout Inventory. On the emotional exhaustion item directly measuring the feeling of being burned out from one's work, only 16 percent of the respondents felt this way once a week or more; most (69 percent) never felt this way or experienced this feeling once a month or less. On the depersonalization item, only 5 percent

TABLE 8.2
Managerial Responses to Selected Burnout Items

Emotional Exhaustion Item (feeling burned out)	Frequency	n
Never to once a month or less	69%	126
A few times a month	15%	28
Once a week to everyday	16%	29
Missing or not applicable	0%	0
Total	100%	183

Depersonalization Item (interacting with probationers as impersonal objects)	Frequency	n
Never to once a month or less	57%	104
A few times a month	4%	8
Once a week to everyday	5%	9
Missing or not applicable	34%	62
Total	100%	183

Personal Accomplishment Item (having an impact on other people's lives)	Frequency	n
Never to once a month or less	20%	36
A few times a month	24%	44
Once a week to everyday	51%	94
Missing or not applicable	5%	9
Total	100%	183

reported frequent feelings of treating probationers as impersonal objects. On the personal accomplishment item, 20 percent (N = 36) reported infrequent feelings of "positively influencing other people's lives through my work" whereas 51 percent felt such positive feelings at least once a week. In summary, most managers reported that they were doing well; only a minority reported feeling burned out.

Managers were queried about selected job attitudes that the burnout literature (e.g., Cherniss, 1980a, 1980b) had noted as sources of job burnout; their responses are summarized in Table 8.3. In the survey instrument, the managers answered these items on a five-point scale ranging from strongly agree to strongly disagree; Table 8.3 shows only the percentage of respondents who agreed with each item; the percentages were calculated only for those who responded to the item in question. Line officer responses are included for comparison purposes, as are significance levels (.05 or better by X^2) for differences between administrators and supervisors.

TABLE 8.3
Managerial Job Attitudes

Job Attitudes	All	Adms.	Sups.	Line POs	Signif.[a]	Missing
Career satisfaction	78%	80%	74%	54%	ns	1
Agency satisfaction	73%	79%	65%	61%	ns	0
Pay satisfaction	36%	36%	35%	25%	ns	0
Satisfaction with promotional opportunities	9%	10%	9%	5%	ns	0
Autonomy	89%	94%	83%	86%	.04	0
Variety	96%	100%	90%	88%	.005	0
Participation in policy making	84%	93%	72%	31%	.0004	0
Participation[b]	73%	79%	65%	47%	.049	8
Role conflict[1]	60%	66%	52%	71%	ns	51
Role conflict[2]	61%	66%	56%	35%	ns	0
Role conflict[3]	89%	90%	86%	78%	ns	0
Quantitative overload	56%	64%	46%	54%	.03	0
Qualitative overload	51%	56%	45%	60%	ns	5
Task feedback	78%	77%	79%	78%	ns	0
Feedback from supervisors	47%	45%	49%	49%	ns	27
Role clarity[1]	96%	97%	94%	96%	ns	1
Role clarity[2]	58%	56%	59%	61%	ns	2
Gun item	4%	1%	7%	7%	ns	18
Assistance with marital problem item	4%	4%	4%	5%	ns	62

[a]Significance findings refer to X^2 differences between administrators and direct supervisors.

[b]The second participation item read, "Supervisors try to get ideas and opinions from officers before making decisions."

Role Conflict[1] measured helping versus monitoring.

Role Conflict[2] measured intersender conflict.

Role Conflict[3] measured agreement re "can't satisfy everybody at the same time."

Role Clarity[1] read, "I know what I have to do on my job."

Role Clarity[2] measured the extent of rules and regulations for job duties.

Examination of Table 8.3 shows that most managers reported satisfaction both with their careers and with their employing agencies. However, one-fifth of the administrators and one-fourth of the supervisors were either dissatisfied with or uncertain of their satisfaction with their careers, and one-fifth of the administrators and one-third of the supervisors reported dissatisfaction or uncertain satisfaction with their employing agencies. There were problems on two economic issues; only one-third of both groups were satisfied with their pay, and only 10 percent were satisfied with the availability of promotional opportunities.

Tangible issues, however, were not the only problematic areas. Although almost all the managers reported satisfactory levels of autonomy and variety in their jobs, many reported experiencing feelings of role conflict. Specifically, about two-thirds of the respondents agreed that the perennial conflict between an emphasis on assistance versus an emphasis on control is still a problem in probation work (i.e., they agreed, "one of the most difficult things about being an officer is trying to be a helper and also trying to be a person who monitors the conditions of probation"). More abstractly, the respondents reported experiencing intersender role conflict; that is, about two-thirds agreed that "[T]o satisfy some people on my job, I have to upset others," and 90 percent agreed with the statement, "[O]n my job I can't satisfy everybody at the same time." About two-thirds of the administrators and 46 percent of the supervisors reported being overloaded with too much work ("I never seem to have enough time to get everything done on my job"). About 50 percent of the managers reported qualitative overload (i.e., agreed, "[G]iven the level of resources in this office, some of my tasks just cannot be done well").

Concerning feedback, over three-fourths of the respondents did experience task feedback (i.e., they agreed, "[E]ven if no one tells me, I can figure out how well I am doing on my job"), but only about half felt that feedback from supervisors was sufficient (i.e., agreed with the statement, "[S]upervisors usually let me know how well I am doing on my job"). Almost all the managers were clear about their role (i.e., they agreed, "[M]ost of the time I know what I have to do on my job"), part of which may be attributable to the presence of rules and regulations "concerning almost everything that comes up." Over half the managers assented to this last item, a result not unexpected in a bureaucratic setting such as probation (McCleary, 1978).

As might be expected, almost all the agency administrators (93 percent) reported involvement in policy decision making, whereas fewer supervisors (72 percent) reported such involvement. Seventy-nine percent of the administrators and 65 percent of the supervisors agreed that "[S]uperiors try to get ideas and opinions from officers before making decisions," whereas only 47 percent of the line officers agreed with this statement, and only 31 percent of the nine officers reported involvement in policy decision making.

Finally, only 4 percent of the respondents advocated carrying a gun to impress probationers with officer authority; arguably, more might agree on carrying a gun for safety purposes. On an item included to attempt to measure a subject's assistance orientation, only 4 percent agreed with the noninterventionist position of allowing a probationer to work out marital problems alone.

DISCUSSION

The findings show that burnout and job dissatisfaction are not pervasive and crisis-level problems among probation managerial personnel. Most administrators and direct supervisors reported that feelings of burnout occurred only infrequently, about 75 percent were satisfied with their careers, and 79 percent of the administrators and 65 percent of the supervisors were satisfied with their employing agencies. Caution is needed, however, because important proportions of both administrators and supervisors reported some job burnout and/or some job dissatisfaction. About 16 percent reported feeling burned out once a week or more, 5 percent reported impersonal treatment of probationers, and about 20 percent reported infrequent feelings of personal accomplishment. Similarly, about 15 percent reported both career and agency dissatisfaction, and about 10 percent were undecided about their satisfaction.

Job dissatisfaction may be even more of a problem for several reasons. First, there is the possibility that some dissatisfied workers may have left the field and are not represented in the results. Second, research on job satisfaction has indicated a tendency to respond favorably to satisfaction questions as a defense against searching personal questions about why workers stay in a negative job (Robinson, Athanasiou, & Head, 1978). This is in accord with cognitive dissonance theory (Festinger, 1957), which holds that people modify either behavior or attitudes to achieve consistency. Third, workers in other occupations report greater satisfaction than the probation managerial personnel reported (Quinn & Staines, 1979).

The low burnout levels seem to be related to three factors. First, 89 percent of the probation managers had at least five years of experience in probation work, and burnout is considered more likely in the incipient stages of one's career (Cherniss, 1980a, 1980b). Second, although client contact is considered to be a critical source of burnout (Maslach, 1976, 1982), 42 percent of the managers reported no client contact, and 31 percent reported fewer than ten hours of client contact in a typical week. Thus, the Maslach Burnout Inventory may be more appropriate for studying line officers than managers, many of whom reported no client contact. As shown in Table 8.1, depersonalization and personal accomplishment scores could not be calculated for about 40 percent of the managerial personnel because they did not answer one or more items that were inapplicable to their noncontact jobs. Emotional exhaustion scores could be calculated for 91 percent of the managers, and 100 percent answered the one item about feeling burned out. Consequently, the Maslach Burnout Inventory seems to have some, but not complete, validity for measuring burnout among managers. A third possible explanation for the low levels of burnout among the managers is that they reported high levels of job satisfaction, autonomy, variety, and participation, all of which, if lacking, are important sources of burnout (Cherniss, 1980a, 1980b).

That managerial personnel reported higher job satisfaction than line personnel and that administrators reported greater satisfaction than supervisors, although not to a statistically significant degree, is consistent with the social psychological literature on job satisfaction, which has consistently found a direct relationship between satisfaction and occupational level (Katz & Kahn, 1978). The job satisfaction literature has found that such variations by occupational level reflect the fact that higher status jobs involve work that is more varied, complex, and challenging. This is supported by the present findings that administrators reported significantly greater autonomy, variety, and participation in decision making than did supervisors, who, in turn, reported about the same autonomy and variety as, but greater participation in decisions than, line officers.

Dissatisfaction with pay and with promotional opportunities are conspicuous complaints among both administrators and supervisors — and, of course, line officers. What can be done about these matters in an era of governmental fiscal constraints is not clear, but ignoring a problem seldom results in improvement. The problem of limited promotional opportunities is probably less critical for administrators than for supervisors (and line officers) because administrators have risen to the top of their field. For both first-line supervisors and line officers, however, the opportunities for career development and career ladders must be explored.

That 60 percent of the managers agreed that a conflict between service and surveillance (assistance and control) still exists in probation suggests that the time is right for mission reform in probation. Rather than continue to operate probation as a confused mixture of assistance and control, it would be more effective to reconceptualize probation in terms of retribution (Barkdull, 1976), risk control (Clear & O'Leary, 1983), the justice model (Fogel, McAnany, & Thomson, 1980), or a reparative sentence (Galaway, 1983). These and similar proposals call for less emphasis on rehabilitation and increased attention to punishment, incapacitation, and consideration of crime victims (for a more complete discussion of this issue, see Chapter 11). It is clear that such reconceptualization and actual implementation would have positive effects on both line officers and managerial personnel. For example, whereas probation's traditional rehabilitation focus seems to have had little influence on recidivism (e.g., Martinson, 1974; Petersilia et al., 1985), a risk control focus, a justice focus, or an emphasis on restitution might be more productive and thus contribute to improved employee satisfaction, an increased sense of personal accomplishment, and decreased feelings of burnout. Both Maslach (1976, 1982) and Cherniss (1980a, 1980b) contend that human service workers are seeking a sense of efficacy, so an attempt at mission reform could offer benefits for employees and also satisfy a public that is less and less tolerant of probation as leniency.

The findings also suggest that managerial personnel should reconsider their practices concerning line officers. The finding that 79 percent of the administrators and 65 percent of the supervisors reported that "[S]uperiors try to get ideas and opinions from officers before making decisions" whereas less than half the line officers reported such consultation suggests several interpretations. One, managers may not be consulting line personnel as much as they think they are. This reasoning is corroborated by the item on policy decision making; only about one-third of the line officers reported involvement in the policy process. A second possibility is that managers only involve a few subordinates in policy decision making; thus, many officers may not be involved in any decisions, but some officers may be involved in most decisions. A third interpretation is that managers accept officer input as information but frequently establish policies in contradiction to officer advice, and officers interpret this as lack of involvement in policy making. In any case, real or perceived neglect of line officer input is a matter of concern because managerial control is often tenuous; that is, managers may be enunciating policy decisions that are either distorted or ignored at the street level (McCleary, 1978). If line workers were more involved, or felt more involved, in the policy process, there might be realistic hope for mission reform, and such mission reform proposals might not simply lie dormant in scholarly journals but actually see whole-hearted implementation.

A Qualitative Analysis of Employee Attitudes 9

Previous chapters have presented detailed, quantitative analyses of officer and managerial burnout. The questionnaire described in Chapter 5 also included considerable space at the end for the officers to make open-ended comments explaining or elaborating on any fixed responses. Officers were requested to "feel free to describe any stress or 'burnout' problems [they] have previously encountered on the job and tell how these problems might be alleviated or prevented."

This chapter presents an analysis of the responses of the approximately 400 probation and parole employees who made open-ended comments. The analysis categorizes the comments and gives representative examples. The chapter also compares and contrasts these qualitative results with the quantitative results presented in Chapters 5, 6, 7, and 8.

This qualitative analysis is important for several reasons. First, an examination of the actual comments of the workers gives a direct view of employee attitudes without the possible distorting effects of forcing answers to questions devised by researchers. Second, such a qualitative analysis gives a slightly different picture of probation/parole worker burnout. Third, given the important role probation and community supervision have played in corrections in the past and the potential role they could play in the future to ameliorate prison overcrowding and obviate the need for further prison construction, what workers themselves have to say is important because both line officers and managers are critical determiners of actual correctional practice, independent of what experts and first-level administrators would prefer probation and parole to be (McCleary, 1978).

METHODOLOGY

The author and a graduate assistant[1] first rated the comments in terms of the apparent extent of job burnout and job dissatisfaction being experienced by the respondents. Then the comments were categorized. More specifically, we rated the open-ended responses on a five-point scale ranging from not burned out at all, somewhat positive, neither burned out nor positive, somewhat burned out, to very burned out. We examined the responses to see if the respondents noted feeling burned out, exhausted, cynical, impersonal, frustrated, or other emotions related to the three aspects of burnout described in previous chapters. A similar five-point scale was used to judge job satisfaction ranging from very dissatisfied to very satisfied. Here the focus was on the worker's overall evaluation of the job. Examination of the comments also indicated that common themes existed, similar to the themes noted in the analysis of Alabama probation and parole officers discussed in Chapter 10 (see also, Whitehead & Lindquist, 1985). Thus, we read the comments a second time to place them in the categories described below.

Some quantitative measures (discussed in Chapter 5) of the job burnout and the job satisfaction of the commenters were also included. This allowed us to compare and contrast the qualitative findings with the quantitative findings and allowed comparison of the commenters with the noncommenters.

FINDINGS

Demographic Findings

Of the 400 respondents who offered open-ended comments on the questionnaire, 77 percent (N = 309) were probation officers, including trainees, aides, and interns, or parole officers, and 21 percent (N = 84) held administrative titles such as supervisor, chief probation officer, or director.[2] The rest of the respondents were clerical workers or court liaison personnel.

As indicated for the entire sample (see Chapter 5), the subsample was predominantly white (96 percent) and male (57 percent). The mean age for the subsample was 34.9 years; respondents ranged from 21 to 68 years with almost 60 percent between 25 and 35 years of age.

About half the commenters (48 percent) had worked in probation for more than five years; about 10 percent had been on the job one year or less.

The bulk of the respondents (87 percent, N = 347) were from New York and Indiana with 13 percent (N = 53) from Pennsylvania and Connecticut.

For those respondents who reported direct client contact, the mean number of weekly client contact hours was about 15; 36 percent (N = 128) had 20 or more hours of face-to-face contact per week; 44 percent (N = 160) had between 10 and 19 hours per week.

Table 9.1 presents information on some of the demographic and job-related variables for those workers who offered open-ended comments and those who did not. The only major difference between the two sets of workers was gender: 44 percent of the commenters but only 32 percent of the noncommenters were female. The other statistically significant differences (weekly contact hours: 14.9 for the commenters and 16.2 for the noncommenters; age: 34.9 for the commenters and 36.4 for the noncommenters) were not substantial enough to warrant attention. In general, workers who offered comments were very similar to workers who refrained; thus, although the commenters are not a random sample and are not as representative of probation officers in general as are the 968 respondents to the structured questionnaire, the commenters are not so distinct from the noncommenters to discount their open-ended responses.

TABLE 9.1
Comparison of the Demographic and Job Characteristics of Commenters and Noncommenters

Characteristic	Commenters	Non-Commenters	Significance
Age	34.9	36.4	.02
% Female	43.5%	32.4%	.02
Seniority			
% 0-2 years	20%	17%	ns
% over 2 years to 5 years	32%	29%	ns
% over 5 years	48%	54%	ns
Weekly client contact hours	14.9	16.2	.02
Caseload (adults)	44.0	41.8	ns
Caseload (juveniles)	11.6	10.9	ns

Note: Significance determined by oneway analysis of variance or by chi-square.

Substantive Findings

As previously noted, the comments of the respondents were rated on a five-point scale to determine each worker's extent of burnout and job satisfaction. Of 322 respondents (80.5 percent of the commenters), from whose comments we could judge the level of burnout, 61 percent (N = 197) were either somewhat or very burned out. Of 320 respondents 62 percent (N = 198) were either somewhat or very dissatisfied with their jobs.

Comparisons of the ratings of worker comments with the quantitative measures of burnout and satisfaction showed some interesting results. Table 9.2 shows mean burnout and intrinsic job satisfaction scores for those employees who offered comments. Examination of this table indicates low levels of burnout. Respondents were experiencing feelings of exhaustion and depersonalization about once a month or less and positive feelings of personal accomplishment and intrinsic job satisfaction slightly more than once a week.[3] Table 9.3 presents responses for key individual items of the Human Services Survey and for the one-item measure of job satisfaction. Although the assessments of burnout and job dissatisfaction based on the open-ended comments of the officers indicated that almost two-thirds of the commenters could be said to be burned out or dissatisfied, the findings listed in Table 9.3 indicate lower levels of these problems. However, rather generous cutoff points were used in the assessments of the open-ended

TABLE 9.2
Mean Burnout and Intrinsic Job Satisfaction Scores for Commenters

Variable	M	SD
Emotional Exhaustion (f)	2.42	1.15
Emotional Exhaustion (i)	3.76	1.40
Depersonalization (f)	1.81	1.19
Depersonalization (i)	2.81	1.55
Personal Accomplishment (f)	4.14	0.86
Personal Accomplishment (i)	4.87	0.86
Intrinsic Job Satisfaction (f)	4.23	1.14
Intrinsic Job Satisfaction (i)	4.87	1.04

Note: n for the commenters varied from 372 to 414.
(f) = frequency dimension; (i) = intensity dimension.

comments; if similarly generous criteria are used with the quantitative measures, the assessments become rather similar. For example, 57 percent of the commenters reported feeling "burned out" at least once a month; 33 percent of the commenters reported depersonalized treatment of the clients at least once a month; and 45 percent of the commenters were dissatisfied or uncertain about their satisfaction with their careers in probation/parole.[4]

The open-ended responses were also reviewed for the purpose of ascertaining various positive and negative aspects of the job. Of these positive and negative job aspects, three major problem areas were listed most frequently. Overload (e.g., too many clients, too much paperwork) was the most frequently listed area of concern with 24 percent (N = 96) of the respondents mentioning it. One of the most bitter comments came from a New York probation officer discussing overload and the related problems it caused:

> The emphasis is on turning out the paper in the name of "accountability" at the expense of serving the needs of the people we're responsible for (the probationers and the community). I'm supposed to keep my desk neat, avoid any attention to detail, and pump out 30 quarterly reports a month. [This bureaucracy] has lost sight of its function and is concerned only with its maintenance needs. Hence, the emphasis on accountability.

Another probation officer from Connecticut expressed concern that perhaps overload was the basis for the problem of role conflict: "We're overloaded with paper and the philosophy is turning to law enforcement rather than helping others which makes things uncomfortable." Another New York officer was concerned not only with the numbers, but the types of people directed into the probation system:

> convicted persons are "dumped" on probation, when their problems really required more intensive supervision and rehabilitation than probation can provide. Although many probationers benefit from probation supervision, those who are placed on probation without any regard to their ability or desire to comply are a major source of tension and frustration to the officer.

Problems with administration (e.g., not enough feedback, no input in decision making) made up the next most frequently listed negative aspect with 24 percent (N = 94) answering in the affirmative. A female probation officer from New York expressed her views about administration in this manner: "People who are in supervisory positions do not attempt to explain procedures or rules ... until one 'fouls up' or 'makes a wrong move.'" A

TABLE 9.3
Responses of Commenters to Selected Burnout Items and to the Job Satisfaction Item

Item	Commenters
Emotional Exhaustion Item	
(feeling burned out)	
Seldom[a]	59%
Occasionally	17%
Frequently	24%
n	417
Depersonalization Item	
(impersonal treatment of clients)	
Seldom[a]	80%
Occasionally	11%
Frequently	9%
n	394
Personal Accomplishment Item	
(impact on people's lives)	
Seldom[a]	20%
Occasionally	27%
Frequently	53%
n	418
Job Satisfaction Item	
("All in all, I would say I am satisfied with my career in probation/parole.")	
Agree	55%
Undecided	23%
Disagree	22%
n	412

[a]Seldom = never to once a month or less; occasionally = a few times a month; frequently = once a week to everyday.

probation officer from Connecticut was even more harsh in his views on administration:

> Management and judicial authorities are not responsive to our problems. They say they are, but nothing ever seems to improve . . . I really think management and moreover legislators, in charge of the purse strings, see us as a necessary evil and don't really care if we are truly performing. Our statistics are much more important to them. Today a district supervisor called and said, "Our total restitution so far for the month is $37,000 — push for $40,000." That is demoralizing.

Another probation officer from Connecticut offered an ironic criticism: "Sometimes you (I) feel like the ancient Hebrews who, when they asked for time off, were told by Pharaoh to make bricks without straw seeing they must have so much free time." Such negative criticisms are important because burnout theory (Cherniss, 1980a, 1980b) posits that lack of consideration from management is an important source of the problem. Thus, it is hardly surprising that workers would be burned out if they reported the following perception offered by a Connecticut officer: "The caseload keeps going up, budgets are being cut back, no new help is hired, and people leave due to attrition — the expectation remains the same: to do everything required, no matter how much work comes in."

The third most frequently listed problem was extrinsic factors (pay, hours, promotions), mentioned by 22 percent (N = 86) of the respondents. Several of the respondents were very emphatic in their comments concerning this area, such as one New York respondent who wrote: "I feel there is definitely a lack of respect for . . . probation officers. Part of the reason is due no doubt to the low salaries paid to probation officers in a society that tends to judge people by the amount of money they earn." Another New York respondent was just as disillusioned: "we are expected to work for wages which are often in fact, below the level which federal government guidelines have established as 'poverty.'" Many respondents were angry that the pay scale was not commensurate with the responsibilities of the job. An Indiana juvenile probation officer wrote: "I am asked to assume a tremendous responsibility: the control of another person's life, but I . . . am trained and paid subject to the whims of my particular county."

Other areas noted by respondents, although not as frequently, were, first, problems with courts or judges, mentioned by 11 percent (N = 43) of the respondents. A New York probation officer expressed serious concern on this point:

> Basically I feel probation is abused by the legal profession, judges, DA's, and attorneys who set themselves up as experts in probation and social work when it is to their convenience. I find it actually painful to see the inconsistencies in sentences that occur every day and know full well that one person goes to jail and another is placed on probation simply based on the mix of personalities

> involved. God help the person that gets into the system unprepared and naive.

Problems with coworkers represented the next most frequently noted problem; 10 percent (N = 39) of the workers noted this difficulty. The most bitter comment relating to this problem came from a female probation officer from Indiana:

> What *does* burn me out is the inner office politics, nit-picking, and back-biting — the notion that we are a team united in a crusade to save the world, and the criticism one receives for not buying into this support system. I am weary to my bones from fighting against the stereotype of the "dedicated, over-worked, underpaid" social worker and from refusing the guilt that is pushed on me by not being that.

The last problem area expressly mentioned in the comments was that of problems with clients; 7 percent (N = 29) mentioned this matter. For example, a New York probation officer with only nine months on the job said:

> The greatest understanding gap is why probationers commit new crimes. The burnout symptoms occur upon violation — where did I fail? Therein lies the explanation for the hardening of the attitudes. I cannot supervise them 24 hours a day, 7 days a week — the assumption of probation is that with authoritative guidance, *they* can overcome their disabilities.

An Indiana respondent described essentially the same complaint: "I generally describe probation work as 'dealing in frustration.' We seldom see our successes; they just disappear into the community. It is our failures that we see all the time." Another New York respondent offered a different complaint about clients: "probation officers seem to be considered as machines. Both the clients and our employers seem to think that we are not entitled to have our own feelings, and certainly personal problems are not allowed."

The respondents were not quite as vocal when looking at the positive aspects of their jobs. Only 3 percent (N = 13) were satisfied with extrinsic job factors; similarly, 3 percent (N = 13) felt that working with clients was a positive aspect of the job; however, 16 percent (N = 64) did say that they felt confident of their ability to do a good job.

DISCUSSION

Based on this qualitative analysis of probation worker comments to the job burnout survey, several conclusions can be drawn. First, the officers studied in this report were more interested in commenting on the negative aspects of their jobs than the positive aspects; they were very concerned with administrative problems, salaries, courts and judges, coworkers, and clients. On the one hand, this may simply be a reflection of the wording of the question, which asked them to "describe any stress or burnout problems you have personally encountered on the job and tell how these problems might be alleviated or prevented." On the other hand, this emphasis on negative aspects of the job may reflect the fact that such problems are more frequent, intense, and noticeable to probation workers than are the positive aspects of the job.

Second, as much of the research on police stress (see, e.g., Kroes, Margolis, & Hurrell, 1974) and correctional officer stress (Cheek & Miller, 1983; Lombardo, 1981; Whitehead & Lindquist, 1986) (see Chapter 10) has noted, probation/parole employees also appear to be very concerned with matters such as the administration and courts. Specifically, 24 percent of the officers mentioned various problems with administration, and another 11 percent mentioned lack of consideration from judges. Concern with such matters was somewhat unexpected in the early police and correctional officer stress research; many had predicted that danger and isolation might be the areas of predominant concern. The concern of probation/parole workers with administrative and court matters is also unexpected from Maslach's (1982) perspective, which contends that client contact is the greatest source of job burnout, whereas concern about administrative and court issues is quite congruent with Cherniss's (1980a, 1980b) perspective, which emphasizes the importance of organizational variables. Officers were indeed concerned about clients; workers listed overload, including the overload of too many clients, as a source of job burnout, and they mentioned other client-related problems such as failure on supervision as distressing. But that overload also included too much paperwork and that administrative and court problems were also very upsetting are more supportive of Cherniss's theory of job burnout than Maslach's for probation workers.

The lesser impact of client contact as a source of burnout for probation officers may be a reflection of the nature of the work; that is, as mentioned previously, probationers and parolees often avoid officers (McCleary, 1978) and limit their mandatory contacts to contacts that are "amiable, superficial, and brief" (Stanley, 1976, p. 97). Such contacts are not the stressful, emotionally laden contacts that Maslach (1982) had in mind when she posited contact to be the major cause of the burnout syndrome. Furthermore, offender contact is only part of the job of probation and parole officers; that officers spend less than 20 hours a week in direct contact with probationers means that there is simply not enough contact to be as problematic as Maslach envisioned.

Worker concerns over administrative and court-related problems indicate that intervention efforts need to be quite different for probation and parole officers than for other human service workers. Whereas Maslach (1982) suggests reducing client contact as a means of reducing or preventing burnout for human service workers, this research and the probation/parole literature indicate that such a direction would be misguided for community corrections personnel. Rather, ameliorative efforts should focus on the administrative and court-related concerns of the officers, including such bread-and-butter matters as pay. Two specific suggestions are in order. First, administrators have to take line officers seriously. Probation officers cannot and should not be put in the position of the correctional officers described by Cheek and Miller (1983) who, like a popular comedian, receive no respect. When fewer than 50 percent of line probation officers feel that "superiors try to get ideas and opinions from officers before making decisions" (see Chapter 8), something is amiss. Superiors ignore line officer input at the price of decreased organizational effectiveness. Second, judges need to be aware of officer complaints and suggestions. Here probation managers can be of service by either communicating officer perceptions to judges or by arranging for meetings between judges and officers. Administrators can advocate such meetings on the basis of mutual benefit; judges and officers alike can communicate their perceptions and suggestions so that both parties can profit.

Third, our rating of the extent of job burnout and job dissatisfaction indicated that both problems were quite prevalent; about 60 percent of the respondents indicated such difficulties. As previously noted, such high levels of these two phenomena may be the result of rather generous cutoff points or of the wording of the instructions for completing the open-ended material. Thus, different cutoff points and more quantitative measures indicate burnout and job dissatisfaction to be less problematic. The negative picture given in the open-ended comments, however, may be more veridical. That is, perhaps a strictly quantitative methodology that reports burnout to be a problem for 20 percent of the officers in an agency (see Chapter 5) is falsely reassuring. Perhaps qualitative approaches such as in-depth interviews or participant observation are needed to assess burnout levels accurately. As noted previously, Clear (1985), for example, has made the claim that probation "is seen as an early-career position which most people eventually leave to take other jobs. Few people stay in community corrections work for their entire careers. . . . Turnover is often high, so-called 'burnout' is epidemic and work world cynicism seems to pervade the office" (p. 40). Job burnout in probation is a problem that cannot be ignored without losing capable and talented workers.

Finally, any examination of burnout would be incomplete without some further mention of the ferment in reconceptualizing the mission of probation, in particular, and community supervision, in general. Given much of the negative evaluation research in community corrections (see, e.g., the Rand study conducted by Petersilia et al., 1985), it is not surprising that some workers have been affected. Although other research (e.g., Vito, 1986) has been much more positive than the Rand study, negative findings can make line officers feel frustrated and incompetent if they feel they are operating in ineffective organizations. Thus, probation and community supervision are facing a challenge. Either they can continue as lenient and meaningless forms of correctional intervention or they can be changed.

As noted, some have suggested that such change should take the form of extreme paring down or separation of functions such that the assistance dimension of probation be left to community social service agencies while "probation officers" or the police focus only on court reports and offender monitoring (Conrad, 1982; Rosecrance, 1986). Others argue that probation should clarify its mission from a murky mixture of assistance and control to a clear focus on risk control (O'Leary & Clear, 1984) or justice (McAnany, Thomson, & Fogel, 1984). Some of these theoretical arguments have already started to influence practice, as evidenced by the current return to intensive supervision (Byrne, 1986; Erwin, 1986, 1987) and the search for new methods such as house arrest (Petersilia, 1986).

This is not the place to evaluate the relative merits of these and other probation mission reform proposals. Two points, however, can be stated here. First, the positive responses of officers to Maslach's personal accomplishment items such as dealing effectively with offender problems indicate that officers enjoy the so-called assistance dimension of the job. Thus, suggestions of Conrad (1982) and Rosecrance (1986) to eliminate this dimension of probation work appear to be misguided from the perspective of the employees. Second, if any reformulation of probation mission and concomitant operations can result in more effective functioning, then such a reformulation should have positive consequences on line officers who seek a sense of efficacy (Cherniss, 1980b). If community supervision does not change its mission and its operations, then many of the "good people," whom even Martinson (1974) noted as being critical in probation, will leave, and the words of a female Indiana officer may well describe the sentiments of those who stay:

> I do not suffer from any illusions about my job — I do not believe the system works — therefore, I don't feel probation works from the standpoint that our intervention actually makes any significant changes in a person's life. However, I am able to accept the limitations and imperfections for now and work within the system from a realistic standpoint.

NOTES

1. Susan Gunn at the University of Alabama at Birmingham assisted in the qualitative analysis of the data.

2. We had 421 respondents offer at least some comment, but we judged 21 comments to be too brief to be informative. However, we did include all 421 commenters in some of our comparisons on the assumption that a person who made any comment at all was more similar to the more verbose commenters than to respondents who offered no comments. Also, pairwise deletion of missing cases resulted in varying sample sizes for various variables of interest.

3. The noncommenters reported very similar mean burnout and job satisfaction scores. The only significant differences between the two were in the emotional exhaustion scores; the noncommenters reported slightly less frequent (2.19) and less intense feelings (3.42) of this aspect of burnout than did the commenters.

4. The responses of the noncommenters were quite similar; 53 percent reported feeling "burned out" at least once a month, 32 percent reported depersonalized treatment of clients at least once a month, and 38 percent were either dissatisfied or undecided about their satisfaction with their careers in probation/parole. Such similarity is further evidence that the commenters are not an unrepresentative group.

Burnout among Southern Correctional Officers and Probation and Parole Officers 10

As noted in Chapter 1, recent years have seen increased research attention being focused on correctional officers and their job problems (for a comprehensive review of the literature, see Philiber, 1987). Inspired by this growing body of research and by an early release program in Alabama, a colleague[1] and the author approached the Alabama Department of Corrections in 1984. Our initial intention was simply to determine how the correctional officers assigned to the early release program, called Supervised Intensive Restitution (SIR), were faring. The uniqueness of the program — prison guards were assigned to essentially parole officer roles supervising prisoners "transferred"[2] to community inmate status — caught our research eye. We were curious how the guards would fare in an environment completely different from the prison environment. Also, we planned to study the recidivism rates of the offenders placed in the program although that study never materialized.

Because there were only about 35 correctional officers assigned to the SIR program at the time, we decided to include a sample of prison correctional officers as a comparison group and a sample of the state probation and parole officers as another comparison group. Fortunately, both the Alabama Commissioner of Corrections and the Director of the Board of Pardons and Paroles agreed to the research project. In fact, the Corrections Commissioner allowed us to return a year later to conduct a follow-up study of the SIR officers to see if one year had resulted in any differences in job experiences.

Because a significant part of our research focused on burnout as an indicator of how all three groups of officers were faring, it seems appropriate to present some of the findings from that research in this chapter. This allows a number of comparisons. First, it allows an examination of burnout in a sample of correctional officers that can be compared to the findings on the probation officers presented in Chapters 5 through 9. Thus, this chapter compares burnout levels and sources of burnout in two types of correctional personnel, community corrections and institutional corrections personnel. Second, the findings on the Alabama probation and parole officers constitute a replication and extension of the research on the officers from the Northeast. If the Alabama probation/parole findings support the research in the earlier study, greater confidence can be placed in them. If the Alabama findings are significantly divergent from the findings in the earlier study, that would indicate that the nature, extent, and causes of burnout may vary extensively from state to state or from one region of the country to another.

The chapter presents data on the burnout scores for the three samples of Alabama correctional employees, a path analysis of correctional officer burnout, and a comparison of the Alabama correctional officers and probation and parole officers.

DATA AND METHODS

A questionnaire on job burnout and its hypothesized sources was administered by mail in May 1984 to a random sample (N = 364) of one-third of all line correctional officers (N = 1,094) from each prison and work-release center in the Alabama correctional system. The response rate was 71 percent (N = 258); the number of officers who had no missing values on the items analyzed in this chapter was 220. The same questionnaire was also administered by mail at the same time to all line probation/parole officers (N = 125) employed by the Alabama Board of Pardons and Paroles. The response rate was 86 percent (N = 108). Finally, all 35 SIR officers were administered the same questionnaire during a training session in May 1984; the response rate was 100 percent.[3]

The average age of the institutional correctional officers (prison guards) was 36.7 years; slightly more than 90 percent were male, and about one-third were black. The officers reported spending an average of 31.6 hours a week in direct contact with inmates. Based on information provided by the Department of Corrections, the sample was not significantly different from the total population of line correctional officers.

The average age of the probation/parole officers was 40.1 years. Eighty percent were male, and 7 percent were black. The average seniority was 15.3 years, and the overwhelming majority (92 percent) were college graduates. Officers reported spending an average of 12 hours a week in direct contact with probationer/parolees; average caseload was 122 offenders.

SIR officers reported spending an average of 24 hours per week in direct contact with offenders and had average caseloads of 35 offenders. The SIR officer sample contained more females and college graduates than the correctional officer sample.

Job burnout was measured with the 22-item Human Services Survey explained in Chapter 5. Because the frequency measures of burnout correlate highly with the intensity measures, only the former are reported here.

The job stress measure was the one-item measure developed by Smith and Ward (1983) in their study of police officers in a southeastern city: "How stressful do you consider your job to be?" The job satisfaction measure was the one-item measure from *The 1977 Quality of Employment Survey* (Quinn & Staines, 1979): "All in all, how satisfied would you say you are with your job?" There are limitations inherent regarding the use of one-item measures of job stress and job satisfaction, but their use enabled us to make some of the comparisons reported earlier. The role conflict measure was the eight-item scale developed by Rizzo, House, and Lirtzman (1970), which included such items as, "I receive incompatible requests from two or more people."

Participation in decision making was measured by a four-item scale developed by Vroom (1959) and included such items as, "If I have a suggestion for improving the job setup in some way, it is easy for me to get my ideas across to my supervisor." Social support was measured by the five-item scale developed by Cleary and Mechanic (1983) and included such items as, "Some people have difficulty finding others with whom they can discuss almost any problem they have. To what extent do you have difficulty finding such people?" Reliability scores for all the multiitem measures were satisfactory (above .70).

BURNOUT IN THE THREE SAMPLES OF WORKERS

Table 10.1 shows the burnout scores for the three samples of correctional employees in Alabama at the time of the research: prison guards (correctional officers), probation and parole officers, and correctional officers in the Supervised Intensive Restitution (SIR) program. Examination of the table shows several things. First, it is clear that the SIR officers were experiencing the lowest levels of burnout in the sample. In fact, they even

TABLE 10.1
Mean Burnout, Satisfaction, Stress, and Role Conflict Scores by Job Title

Score	POs	COs	SIR	Sample 1[a]
Emotional exhaustion	2.24	2.17	1.56[b]	2.34
Depersonalization	2.08	2.12	1.73	1.80
Personal accomplishment	4.22	4.09	4.60[c]	4.10
Job satisfaction	2.32	2.12[d]	2.63	n/a[f]
Job stress	2.48	2.14	1.49[b]	n/a[f]
Role conflict	4.57	4.15[e]	4.07	n/a[f]

Note: Higher scores reflect greater values of all the variables. Thus, some variables scored differently than for the correctional officers in Tables 10.2–10.4; *n* for the POs varied from 104 to 108, for the COs from 241 to 258, for the SIR officers from 31 to 35, and for Sample 1 officers from 709 to 725; pairwise deletion used.

[a]Mean burnout scores of line probation officers from NY, IN, & CT, line parole officers from IN, and line probation/parole officers from the Eastern District of PA presented for comparison purposes (see Chapter 5).

[b]SIR officers differed from AL POs and COs (Scheffe test).

[c]SIR officers differed from AL COs (Scheffe test).

[d]COs differed from Al POs and SIR officers (Scheffe test).

[e]COs differed from AL POs (Scheffe test).

[f]Different measures of these phenomena were used for the Sample 1 respondents.

$p < .05$ for Scheffe test comparisons.

reported lower exhaustion and higher accomplishment scores than the northern probation/parole officers. Second, Alabama correctional officers and probation/parole officers were experiencing similar levels of job burnout. Third, the Alabama probation/parole officers reported levels of emotional exhaustion and personal accomplishment quite similar to those reported by the line officers in the sample from the first round of the research — the officers from New York State, Indiana, and Connecticut (z=tests). Depersonalization, however, was significantly higher for the Alabama probation/parole officers compared with their colleagues in the North. Fourth, the correctional officer exhaustion score was lower, and the depersonalization score was higher than were the northern probation and parole officer scores.

Discussion of Findings on Extent of Burnout

Two points stand out in these findings in light of what has gone before. First, that the Alabama probation/parole officers reported levels of exhaustion and accomplishment very similar to those found in the northern sample suggests that burnout problems are remarkably similar across different regions of the country. Likewise, the similarity in the Alabama probation/parole officer and correctional officer scores suggests that burnout problems are very similar even across different types of correctional employment. Thus, it may be that probation/parole employment is more similar to prison employment than has been considered. If further research corroborates this finding, then strategies designed to improve working conditions in either setting may be appropriate for the other to a greater extent than previously considered.

The second major finding was the low levels of burnout among the correctional officers in Alabama's Supervised Intensive Restitution program. An initial reaction to this finding was that perhaps some sort of Hawthorne effect was at work. In other words, we considered the possibility that the 35 SIR officers were in a new program that was very dear to the Commissioner of Corrections at the time and thus were receiving a great deal of attention as favored sons in an innovative effort. We knew that the commissioner was very fond of the program and wanted it to work. Thus, there was the possibility that both he and others in the Department of Corrections were lavishing attention and resources on the program but that the newness would wear off and burnout would increase.

To test this possibility, we retested the SIR officers one year later. Because their burnout scores were very similar to the original scores, we (Lindquist & Whitehead, 1986c, p. 293) concluded that the positive scores were a reflection not of novelty or attention but of job enlargement: "When given an opportunity to play a legitimate role regarding the provision of human services, these officers did perceive a considerable sense of personal accomplishment and job satisfaction." Thus, we found evidence for the claim that guards want to be more than just turnkeys (Johnson, 1987; Lombardo, 1981), and we concluded that such job enlargement could also be implemented within the prison setting as well as in an early release program such as SIR (Lindquist & Whitehead, 1986c).

A MODEL OF CORRECTIONAL OFFICER JOB BURNOUT

Based on a review of the correctional officer literature, as structured by the theoretical perspective outlined in Chapter 3, a model of the job burnout process was constructed for the correctional officers (see Figure 10.1). This model was constructed after examining the contribution of a number of variables, suggested by the literature, in a series of regression equations. Significant predictors were considered for inclusion in the model; others were not. In regard to the latter category, it is interesting that various measures of work assignment, such as shift and type of institution (e.g., prison versus work-release center), did not explain a significant amount of the variance in burnout. Because officers did bid for work assignments in a manner somewhat similar to the process described by Lombardo (1981) in his study of Auburn Prison, it is possible that some officers did bid for jobs to increase or decrease contact with inmates (e.g., being a "rover" in general population or being on an "outside" squad). Our measures did not indicate that the type of work assignment was an important predictor of burnout; whether more precise measures would have provided other results remains an empirical question.

Proceeding from left to right in the model, burnout theorists agree that client contact is the central cause of burnout (see Chapter 2). "For the professional helper, overload translates into too many people and too little time to adequately serve their needs — a situation ripe for burnout" (Maslach, 1982, p. 38). Client contact is stressful because it centers on client problems. These problems are emotionally charged and frequently lead to recommended solutions that are often difficult, if not impossible, to achieve (Maslach & Jackson, 1981). Contact with inmates may be even more stressful than contact with probationers or parolees because of the involuntary nature of the interaction and the danger actually present or perceived to be present in a prison setting (Cheek & Miller, 1983; Lombardo, 1981; Sykes, 1958). As has been aptly phrased, correctional officers are as much imprisoned as their captives, and a very real pain of that imprisonment is interaction with less than desirable persons. Although correctional officers may develop routines to control their nonvoluntary clients (Lipsky, 1980), which may in turn reduce stress, the costs of such control strategies may be increased by client demands.

As noted in Chapter 3, Cherniss (1980b) agrees that excessive client contact is a source of burnout, but he differs from Maslach in that he puts more emphasis on the employing agency and what it can do to mitigate the negative aspects of interaction — such as too many clients in general, lack of time for consultation, and too many clients with extremely intractable problems. Supervisors, for example, can offer support to staff, including technical assistance, assistance in working through the feelings generated by the interaction process, buffers against community groups or government agencies, advocacy for line staff vis-à-vis funding sources, and simple responsiveness (Cherniss, 1980b). Likewise, fellow workers can offer support by discussing problems, volunteering information and advice, providing

FIGURE 10.1 — A Model of the Job Burnout Process for Correctional Officers

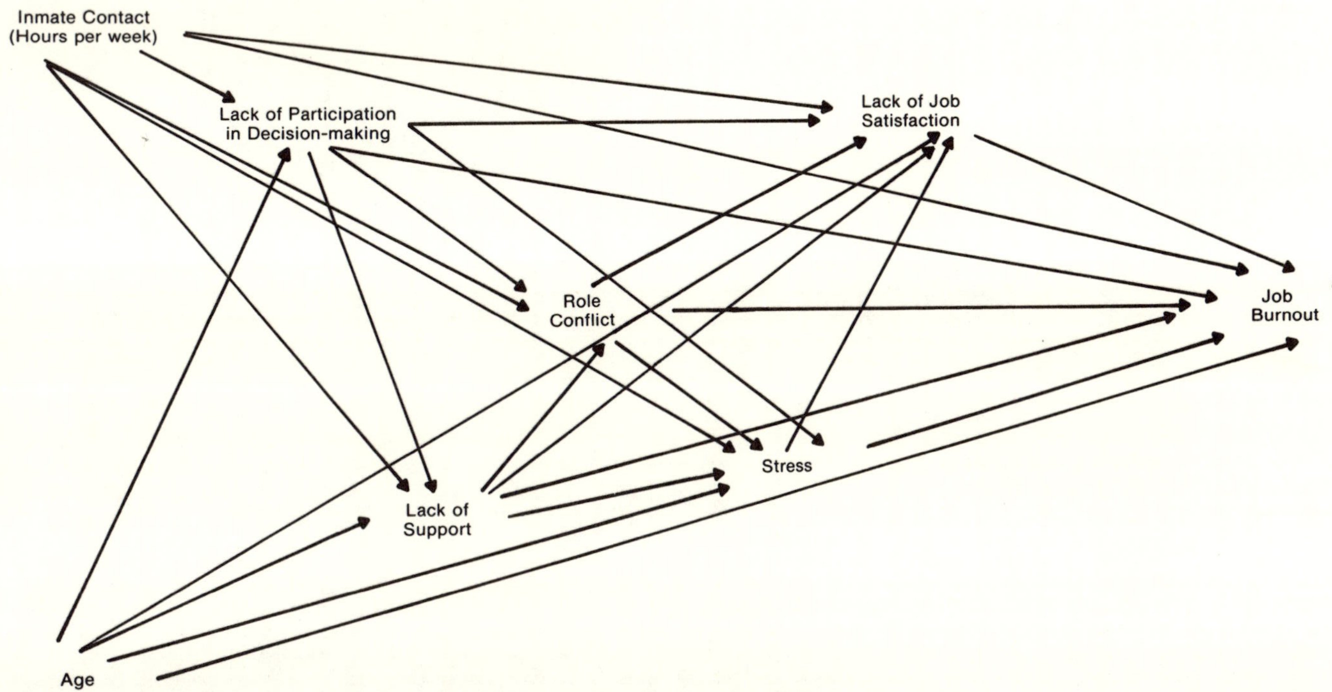

[a]Emotional Exhaustion, Depersonalization, and Lack of Personal Accomplishment.

feedback, offering a united front in any conflicts with management or community groups, and being a source of stimulation: "When one can discuss work experiences with colleagues, those experiences often become more interesting and meaningful" (Cherniss, 1980b, p. 120).

One caveat is that a path model assumes unidirectional relationships, but some of the prior variables in the model may not only affect subsequent variables but, in turn, may be reciprocally affected by such variables. Client contact, for example, may initially cause stress; in turn, such stress may induce officers to withdraw from clients. Our analysis leaves this issue open to further research; longitudinal analysis would probably be the best method for addressing such issues.

The literature on correctional officers echoes Cherniss's emphasis on support. Both Lombardo (1981) and Cheek and Miller (1983) have argued that the primary source of guard stress is their treatment by the administration. As an umbrella term, "administrative" sources of stress cover such matters as the following: lack of clear guidelines for job performance, lack of communication from management, inoperable rules developed by persons unacquainted with the actual work setting, lack of participation in decision making, and lack of administrative support. Cheek and Miller (1983) have named this the "double-bind" theory of correctional officer stress, a predicament noted in other recent research (e.g., Jacobs & Kraft, 1978; Lombardo, 1981; Toch & Klofas, 1982). Although the informal structure of an organization may partially compensate for the effect of administrative stressors and although workers in public service organizations have some resources to resist managerial direction (Lipsky, 1980, pp. 23–25), the intrinsically conflictual nature of worker-management relations appears to generate considerable job stress.

To measure these concerns, scales tapping participation in decision making and role conflict were included in the study. Arguably, participation in decision making will generate greater social support on the job and will reduce the role conflict that is considered to be a central source of burnout (Cherniss, 1980b). The role conflict being measured is the conflict of working in a setting where the line officer feels he or she must balance incompatible demands from different audiences (i.e., management and offenders), perform tasks he or she feels should be done differently, and produce results despite lacking the resources (human and other) to complete assignments. The conflict being measured is not the often mentioned conflict between treatment and custody concerns; that specific type of role conflict is usually not reported by officers as a major source of job stress (Cheek & Miller, 1983; Toch & Klofas, 1982). Although it was assumed that participation in decision making would reduce role conflict, it is recognized that some workers may prefer routinization to a job enlarged by such participation. For these workers, increased participation may exacerbate role conflict and job dissatisfaction (Hulin & Blood, 1968).

Social support can refer to the provision of information and/or emotional assistance either at work or in one's personal life. Support received from both settings has been cited as attenuating burnout (Cherniss, 1980a, 1980b). The measure eventually employed in our study (from Cleary & Mechanic, 1983) probably tapped off-job support more than on-job support because several of the items concerned hypothetical situations regarding availability of support in the middle of the night. However, officers may consider fellow workers to be sources of such support, and the abstract nature of two scale items could very well be interpreted as referring to support from peers or superiors at work. Having noted these caveats, it is hypothesized that support mitigates role conflict, job stress, job dissatisfaction, and burnout.

Age was included in the model because both leading burnout theorists include it in their models. Maslach (1982) has found that younger workers usually score higher on burnout than older workers, a finding similar to that of greater job satisfaction among younger workers and a finding congruent with Maslach's interview data showing that younger workers who are unable to cope may leave human service work altogether (Maslach & Jackson, 1981). Maslach also contends that age is not just an indicator of seniority: "'Older but wiser' seems to be the case here — with increased age, people are more stable and mature, have a more balanced perspective on life and are less prone to the excesses of burnout" (Maslach, 1982, p. 59). Cherniss has noted Maslach's findings on the relationship between age and burnout and has also posited that age may be important as an indicator of experience: "Prior experience with the task, the stressor, and/or the situation attenuates the effects of stress" (Cherniss, 1980b, p. 136).

Thus it is hypothesized that age has attenuating effects on role conflict, stress, job dissatisfaction, and burnout. Age was chosen over seniority as a study variable because of Maslach's argument and because separate analyses showed age to have much stronger effects on the model variables than seniority (age and seniority were correlated at the .50 level). If seniority per se were the paramount factor in determining the outcome of an officer's bid for a particular work assignment, which might have the effect of increasing or decreasing inmate contact, we would have been reluctant to use age as a study variable. However, discussions with correctional administrators indicated that seniority determined work assignments only when the performance ratings and attendance records of two or more bidders were more or less the same; accordingly, the variable with stronger effects (age) was selected.

Job (dis)satisfaction and stress are in the model because "burnout is defined as psychological withdrawal from work in response to excessive stress or dissatisfaction" (Cherniss, 1980b, p. 16). Our consideration of burnout as a response to chronic stress is endorsed by Maslach, but (as noted in Chapter 2) she contends that job dissatisfaction is only moderately correlated with burnout (about .20; Maslach & Jackson, 1981, p. 109). Stress is depicted as a source of job dissatisfaction in the model because stress is a more tangible and immediate problem for workers than is the existence, in a generic sense, of an unpleasurable or negative emotional state resulting from the appraisal of one's job or job experiences (Locke, 1976, p. 1300).

Findings for the Alabama Correctional Officers

Table 10.2 shows the intercorrelations, means, and standard deviations of the study variables. Stress, role conflict, lack of support, lack of job

TABLE 10.2
Intercorrelations, Means, and Standard Deviations of the Model Variables

Variable	2	3	4	5	6	7	8	9	10	M[a]	SD
(1) Age	-.14	-.01	-.19	-.11	-.26	-.13	-.27	-.37	-.08	36.7	10.6
(2) Weekly hours of inmate contact	--	-.15	-.05	-.02	.09	-.14	.02	.02	-.19	31.6	12.5
(3) Lack of participation in decision-making		--	.20	.40	.15	.41	.19	.13	.20	2.55	.68
(4) Lack of support			--	.33	.23	.24	.42	.37	.04	.41	.41
(5) Role conflict				--	.30	.33	.41	.38	.07	4.21	1.30
(6) Stress					--	.23	.49	.32	-.01	2.18	1.39
(7) Lack of job satisfaction						--	.40	.26	.23	.89	.73
(8) Emotional exhaustion							--	.58	.01	2.23	1.25
(9) Depersonalization								--	.05	2.13	1.46
(10) Lack of personal accomplishment									--	1.87	1.06

[a]Higher scores reflect greater emotional exhaustion, depersonalization, stress, role conflict, weekly hours of inmate contact, and age, as well as greater lack of participation in decision making, lack of support, lack of job satisfaction, and lack of personal accomplishment.

$n = 220$; listwise deletion.

satisfaction and age showed the strongest zero-order correlations with the emotional exhaustion and depersonalization aspects of burnout. Lack of participation in decision making was slightly correlated with these two measures of burnout and, unexpectedly, weekly hours of inmate contact showed almost no relationship to exhaustion or depersonalization. Another unexpected finding was the correlation between age and hours of inmate contact; apparently, older workers had assignments with less inmate contact.

Hours of inmate contact did correlate, however, with lack of personal accomplishment; surprisingly, workers who reported more contact also reported more frequent feelings of personal accomplishment. Lack of participation in decision making and lack of job satisfaction were also associated with less frequent feelings of personal accomplishment.

Concerning the hypothesized direct effects, Table 10.3 contains the standardized path coefficients for our model of job burnout. For emotional exhaustion, the strongest direct effects stemmed from stress, lack of job satisfaction, lack of support, and role conflict; all the variables in the model explained 41 percent of the variance. For depersonalization, significant predictors were age, role conflict, lack of support, and stress. All the variables in the model explained 30 percent of the variance. For lack of personal accomplishment, only weekly hours of inmate contact and lack of job satisfaction showed significant direct effects; thus only 7 percent of the variance was explained.

Only role conflict and lack of participation in decision making had any significant direct effects on lack of job satisfaction (.14 and .31, respectively), and only role conflict (.22) and age (–.21) had any significant direct effects on stress. Lack of participation in decision making and lack of support both showed significant direct effects on role conflict. Age and lack of participation in decision making both had significant direct effects on support. Only weekly hours of inmate contact had any direct effect, a small one (–.15), on lack of participation in decision making.

Table 10.4 presents a decomposition of the effects of each variable into its direct, indirect, total, and noncausal effects. Examination of the table shows that lack of job satisfaction, stress, and role conflict had considerable spurious effects on emotional exhaustion, due to their relation to the causally prior variables in the model. Stress, role conflict, and lack of support showed the largest total effects on exhaustion (all about .30); both age and lack of job satisfaction showed total effects of above .20 on exhaustion. Further examination of Table 9.3 shows that lack of participation in decision making exercised its effect on emotional exhaustion in a largely indirect manner — through lack of job satisfaction, role conflict, and lack of support. The effect of age was also mostly an indirect one. The weakest variable was weekly hours of inmate contact; in fact, this variable had almost no relationship to emotional exhaustion. For depersonalization, the largest total effects were those of age, lack of support, and role conflict (all about .30). The other variables showed little causal effect on depersonalization; both stress and lack of job satisfaction showed noteworthy spurious impact (.18 and .17,

TABLE 10.3
Standardized Path Coefficients and Multiple Rs for the Model of Burnout

	3	4	5	6	7	EE[a]	DP[b]	LPA[c]
(1) Age	-.03	-.19*	-.05	-.21*	-.09	-.09	-.26*	-.10
(2) Weekly hours of inmate contact	-.15*	-.05	.04	.07	-.11	.01	-.01	-.16*
(3) Lack of participation in decision-making		.19*	.35*	.05	.31*	-.08	-.07	.13
(4) Lack of support			.25*	.11	.08	.23*	.21*	-.03
(5) Role conflict				.22*	.14*	.19*	.24*	-.02
(6) Stress					.11	.31*	.13*	-.07
(7) Lack of job satisfaction						.23*	.09	.17*
Multiple R	.15	.28*	.48*	.40*	.49*	.66*	.56*	.32*
Adjusted R^2	.01	.07*	.21*	.14*	.22*	.41*	.30*	.07*

Note: When nonsignificant paths were deleted and the model reestimated, only minimal alterations occurred in the parameter estimates, and there were no changes in the significant paths.

$^*p < .05$.

$n = 220$.

[a]Emotional exhaustion.

[b]Depersonalization.

[c]Lack of personal accomplishment.

TABLE 10.4
Decomposition Effects of Model Variables on the Three Aspects of Burnout

	Effects within Model				
	Correlation	Direct	Indirect	Total	Noncausal
EMOTIONAL EXHAUSTION					
Age	-.27	-.09	-.14	-.23	-.04
Weekly hours of inmate contact	.02	.01	.00	.01	.01
Lack of participation in decision-making	.19	-.08	.20	.12	.07
Lack of support	.42	.23	.10	.33	.09
Role conflict	.41	.19	.10	.29	.12
Stress	.49	.31	.03	.34	.15
Lack of job satisfaction	.40	.23	.00	.23	.17
PERSONALIZATION					
Age	-.37	-.26	-.09	-.35	-.02
Weekly hours of inmate contact	.02	-.01	.01	.00	.02
Lack of participation in decision-making	.13	-.07	.16	.09	.04
Lack of support	.37	.21	.08	.29	.08
Role conflict	.38	.24	.04	.28	.10
Stress	.32	.13	.01	.14	.18
Lack of job satisfaction	.26	.09	.00	.09	.17
LACK OF PERSONAL ACCOMPLISHMENT					
Age	-.08	-.10	.00	-.10	.02
Weekly hours of inmate contact	-.19	-.16	-.04	-.20	.01
Lack of participation in decision-making	.20	.13	.04	.17	.03
Lack of support	.04	-.03	.00	-.03	.07
Role conflict	.07	-.02	.01	-.01	.08
Stress	-.01	-.07	.02	-.05	.04
Lack of job satisfaction	.23	.17	.00	.17	.06

Note: For an explanation of these terms, see Nie et al. (1975, pp. 387–89).

respectively). As was the case with emotional exhaustion, inmate contact had no relationship to the depersonalization aspect of burnout. In regard to lack of personal accomplishment, weekly hours of inmate contact, lack of job satisfaction, and lack of participation in decision making had the highest total effects, and most of this effect was direct. The effect of inmate contact, however, was contrary to our expectation in that the more contact reported, the greater the accomplishment reported.

COMPARISON OF ALABAMA COs AND POs

Because the same instrument was also administered at the same time to Alabama probation and parole officers, it is possible to compare the results for the two groups of workers. Because the probation and parole officer sample was smaller (N = 108) than the correctional officer sample, however, it did not seem appropriate to present a full-scale path model. Instead, the burnout measures were simply regressed on the same independent variables as was the case with the correctional officer sample. Given the caution that the sample contained only about 100 probation and parole officers, the results allow some comparing and contrasting of the two samples.

Findings for the Alabama POs

As indicated in Table 10.5, the results of the regression analyses for the probation/parole sample were remarkably similar to the results obtained for the correctional officers. In the emotional exhaustion equation, job stress, job

TABLE 10.5
Regression Results of Burnout Measures on Model Variables: Alabama Probation and Parole Officers

	Emotional Exhaustion		Depersonalization		Personal Accomplishment	
Independent Variables	Beta	t-value	Beta	t-value	Beta	t-value
Age	.10	1.25	-.14	-1.49	.13	1.36
Weekly hours of client contact	.13	1.78	.03	0.36	.22*	2.28
Participation in decision-making	-.05	-0.58	-.01	-0.10	.04	0.35
Support	-.02	-0.24	.07	0.77	-.06	-0.60
Role Conflict	.19*	2.32	.36*	3.51	-.05	-0.50
Stress	.40*	5.17	.15	1.54	-.01	-0.14
Job satisfaction	-.40*	-4.95	-.12	-1.22	.36*	3.48
Adjusted R^2	.50*		.23*		.17*	

Note: Higher scores reflect greater values of all the model variables. Thus, some variables scored differently than for the correctional officers in Tables 10.2–10.4

$n = 96$; listwise deletion used.

*$p < .05$.

satisfaction, and role conflict emerged as significant independent variables. Client contact (hours per week) was not a significant predictor of exhaustion although it did approach statistical significance (actual significance: .08). Role conflict was the only significant independent variable in the depersonalization equation. Concerning personal accomplishment, both client contact and job satisfaction were related significantly to feelings of accomplishment; the greater the contact and the greater the satisfaction, the greater the accomplishment.

DISCUSSION OF FINDINGS ON SOURCES OF BURNOUT

One of the most dramatic findings was a negative one: the lack of influence of inmate contact on two measures of burnout. Contrary to Maslach (1976, 1982), but consistent with the findings discussed in Chapter 6, the correctional officers and the probation/parole officers in Alabama did not associate inmate contact with burnout, in terms of either emotional exhaustion or depersonalization. Furthermore, the effect of contact on the personal accomplishment aspect of burnout was contrary to Maslach's theory; officers who reported greater inmate contact also reported the most frequent feelings of personal accomplishment. Finally, inmate contact had no significant direct effect on such variables as role conflict, stress, or lack of job satisfaction.

The most limited interpretation of this finding is that client contact in prisons and probation/parole is different from client contact in other human service settings. Some support for this interpretation is provided by McCleary's (1978) assertion that correctional clients — specifically, parolees — seek to avoid contact with parole agents or to make any contact as brief and nonintrusive as possible. Parolees, of course, fear revocation and consequently seek to hide negative information from officers. In prison, such avoidance behavior has been considered to be an integral part of the inmate code. If the prisoners in this state were adhering to such a code, it is possible that contact with correctional officers was indeed superficial and hardly stressful; however, in social work settings, client contact may indeed be stressful because such clients do besiege counselors with emotionally laden and difficult problems, as Maslach and Jackson (1981) have described.

Another interpretation is that the variable of weekly hours of inmate contact is too global. Contact per se is not stressful; it is the type of contact that causes problems. Lombardo (1981), for example, found that only dangerous or insulting interaction with inmates was problematic for officers; Cheek and Miller (1983) found concern about violence to be "the most feared and disliked aspect of their jobs" (p. 114). Thus, outside a correctional institution, contact with clients causes concern because it is intensely emotional; within an institution, contact is often superficial and is problematic only in certain circumstances, such as those potentially harmful to the officer. Because instances of physical harm are relatively rare, perhaps Shamir and Drory's (1982) finding no correlation between perception of danger and occupational tedium for Israeli correctional officers was not totally unexpected.

Still another interpretation may relate to Lipsky's (1980) theory of street-level bureaucracy. According to Lipsky, street-level bureaucrats (line workers in public service organizations) develop routines (e.g., rationing services and husbanding resources) to manage their nonvoluntary clients in accordance with worker preferences; these routines then become the policies of public agencies. If correctional officers are routinizing their contact with inmates, such contact, although taking some of the officer's time, may not be perceived as very stressful.

The second dramatic finding was the impact of administrative practices on job stress and burnout. One interpretation of this finding is support for the recently advanced double-bind theory of correctional officer stress. Specifically, Cheek and Miller (1983) contend that officers primarily experience stress through administrative matters such as lack of clear guidelines, lack of participation in decision making, crisis management, inoperable rules, and lack of administrative support; the result is that officers feel that they are in the middle between administrators and inmates, respected by neither. The strong effect of role conflict as measured by the Rizzo, House, and Lirtzman (1970) items (e.g., "I receive incompatible requests from two or more people"; "I have to buck a rule or policy in order to carry out an assignment") provides empirical support for the double-bind theory. Clearly, the guard is often in the position of the popular comedian who gets no respect, "not from the outside community . . . , not from the inmates who use him as a dumping ground for their hostility, not from prison administrators who expect him to play the tin soldier" (Cheek & Miller, 1983, p. 119). Such concern with administrative issues as the overriding source of stress for correctional officers is found in other research on guards, both in the United States (Jacobs & Kraft, 1978; Lombardo, 1981) and in Israel (Shamir & Drory, 1982).

Another interpretation of this finding may, again, relate to Lipsky's (1980) theory of street-level bureaucracy. Whereas client contact may not be very stressful, managerial desire for control and accountability is viewed by Lipsky as conflicting with worker desire for autonomy and discretion. Although workers have some resources for resisting managerial control, administrative policy and practices are, nevertheless, perceived as stressful.

As expected, lack of social support was associated with job burnout for correctional officers; having someone to share problems with may be a positive coping strategy for the individual officer. To be avoided here is any overemphasis on personal coping strategies when burnout stems from such organizational difficulties as role conflict; the problem of burnout does call for individual coping strategies, but

> the most useful point of intervention is the job and work setting. . . . Obviously, the problem cannot be completely eliminated until individuals and the society in which they live are changed, but much can be done before this occurs by changing the structure of roles, power, and norms in human service organizations (Cherniss, 1980b, p. 158).

Although Cherniss (1980b) may have underestimated the difficulty involved in changing organizational structure, especially within a prison, his point is well taken. Prison administrators can encourage correctional officers to seek personal support; however, the development of individual coping strategies may act as a barrier to organizational change. Administrators cannot, therefore, overencourage the development of such strategies; they must accept the responsibility for changing organizational sources of job stress and burnout. As Lipsky (1980, p. 187) has commented:

> People do not readily give up survival mechanisms. This is one of the reasons it is easier to change articulated policy from the top than to change practice from below. Policy articulated from the top is not rooted in defense mechanisms developed to cope with the job, while the policy that emerges from practice is rooted in survival.

As was the case for the probation officers discussed in Chapter 6, age also had considerable influence on burnout; older guards reported lower burnout scores. One possible interpretation for this finding is that such workers learned to cope; another is that the workers who could not cope with the job quit. Either way, the findings support the contention of Toch and Klofas (1982) that officers do mellow as time passes, contrary to the fallacy that older officers contaminate young, liberal, inmate-oriented officers with the cynicism and despair of rampant burnout. Thus the influence of senior officers on their younger peers may well be "a softening, tolerance-inducing and liberalizing one" (Toch & Klofas, 1982, p. 43). As noted in Chapter 6, the findings on the effect of age also suggest that attention be paid to the younger employees so that the reality shock (Kramer, 1974) of the prison environment does not deter them from considering a career in corrections. Such attention might prevent correctional employment from being "an early-career position which most people eventually leave to take other jobs" (Clear, 1985, p. 40). It should also be mentioned that age, as a correlate of seniority, may possibly be associated with successful bids for job assignments requiring less direct inmate contact.

The strong direct relationships between stress and emotional exhaustion and lack of job satisfaction and exhaustion are illuminating because they suggest that factors that heighten either stress or dissatisfaction will also intensify job burnout. In terms of intervention, the findings suggest that research on reducing stress and enhancing job satisfaction can also benefit the employee or the manager seeking to reduce job burnout. This is important because the research on stress and on job satisfaction is both more established and more encompassing than the relatively recent research on burnout. Individual workers, therefore, can benefit from stress reduction techniques (e.g., Brief, Schuler, & VanSell, 1981; Eliot & Bred, 1984; Friedman & Ulmer, 1984); managers, in turn, might consider some of the suggested ways to increase job satisfaction, such as increasing the variety, complexity, and challenge of the job (Katz & Kahn, 1978, p. 364). For example, Brief, Munro, and Aldag (1976) surveyed correctional personnel in a midwestern state and found a significant, positive association between job enlargement and level of job satisfaction. Although we agree with the overall assessment of Perrow (1979) that the case for job enlargement has been overstated, there is some evidence that correctional officers might gain satisfaction from at least one type of job enlargement — expanding the provision of human services to inmates (Johnson, 1977; Lombardo, 1981; Toch & Klofas, 1982). Accordingly, such expansion might be considered by correctional managers.

In conclusion, perhaps the major findings of the research were the importance of administrative practices as sources of job burnout and the minimal effect of undifferentiated inmate contact as a source. This finding and similar, earlier findings of Lombardo (1981) and Cheek and Miller (1983) show a convergence that might encourage correctional administrators to develop an agenda for organizational change. Although the creation of individual coping strategies may ameliorate officer stress, they may also impede organizational change. Accordingly, correctional administrators might consider changing working conditions within prisons both by enlarging the job of the correctional officer and by developing organizational designs to deal with job-related worker problems.

NOTES

1. This research was conducted jointly with Charles A. Lindquist when he and the writer were colleagues at the University of Alabama at Birmingham. Article accounts of the research, which give more detailed information on the history and scope of the program, can be found in Lindquist & Whitehead (1986a, 1986b, 1986c) and Whitehead & Lindquist (1985, 1986, 1987).

2. Technically, the Alabama Department of Corrections considered offenders in the Supervised Intensive Restitution program as "inmates" who had been "transferred" to community custody status. For practical and comparative purposes, the program was an early release program.

3. Because there were only 35 officers in the Supervised Intensive Restitution program, administration of the questionnaire at a training session ensured maximum participation in the survey.

Summary and Implications 11

This research arose as an effort to explore and analyze burnout in probation/parole and institutional corrections. The human services literature indicated that burnout was a very possible problem for people who do "people-work." The corrections literature reported several job problems in community and institutional corrections.

This chapter presents the key findings of the research and suggests implications for intervention and for further research. This presentation is a recapitulation and extension of preliminary discussions of implications.

SUMMARY OF BURNOUT FINDINGS

As noted in Chapter 6, burnout is a problem for some, but certainly not all nor even most, workers in probation and parole. Approximately one of five officers reported frequent feelings of emotional exhaustion, fewer than 10 percent reported feelings of depersonalization, and a minority reported feelings of lack of personal accomplishment. Intriguingly, extremely similar burnout scores were reported by the officers in the separate sample from Alabama conducted three years after the original research. Thus, officers from several states at two points in time reported similar job burnout scores. These findings indicate that most officers are not experiencing the problem but that a sizable minority are having difficulty.

The findings also indicated that simple client contact and heavy caseloads did not in and of themselves cause burnout. Specifically, the path analyses of the probation officer data and also of the correctional officer data indicated that contact had little or no effect on emotional exhaustion and depersonalization and that the effect on personal accomplishment was diametrically opposed to Maslach's burnout theory — greater contact was associated with more frequent feelings of accomplishment. The path analyses showed that problems such as role conflict and lack of participation in decision making were related to burnout. In other words, the findings were consistent with Cherniss's (1980b) model, which stresses organizational sources of burnout.

The separate analysis of gender and burnout indicated that gender was not a strong determinant of burnout but that male and female probation officers were experiencing similar levels of burnout and similar job problems leading to burnout.

The analysis of managerial personnel versus line officers indicated that managers were experiencing fewer problems than line officers. Furthermore, because many managers checked "not applicable" when answering the burnout items, burnout — or the burnout measure — may not be as appropriate for managers as for line workers.

The qualitative analysis of the open-ended responses of the approximately 400 respondents who chose to make comments on the questionnaires indicated two things. First, the open-ended responses indicated that burnout may be more extensive than is indicated by the quantitative measures. This finding is reported cautiously, however, because the instructions for the open-ended responses may have influenced the respondents to focus on negative aspects of the job and because rather generous cutoff points were used. The second suggestion from the qualitative analysis is that the commenters dwelled more on administrative problems in the occupation than on client contact problems. Such findings are contrary to those suggested by Maslach (1982) but congruent with the findings from research on job stress in policing (Kroes et al., 1974) and in prison settings (Cheek & Miller, 1983).

INTERVENTION IMPLICATIONS

The findings suggest several implications for managers, line officers, mission reform, and researchers. These four levels of implications will be addressed respectively.

Implications for Managers

The first implication for managers is to be aware of the possibility of burnout. This may sound obvious, but sometimes the obvious is what people are most likely to neglect. In responding to the request to allow his probation officers to complete the burnout questionnaires, one probation director refused cooperation and said that burnout was simply a faddish term and that he had been in the field for more than 30 years without burning out. The proper response to these objections is that the accumulating research on burnout suggests that it is more than a fad and that a manager's lack of personal difficulty with burnout does not guarantee that his/her employees will not experience the problem.

Thus, managers should be aware of the possibility of burnout. Managers might well conduct periodic burnout "checkups" (Cherniss, 1980a) or at least be attuned to the possibility of the problem:

> "Consciousness-raising" must be the first step in any effort to deal with the problem of burnout in a community agency. If supervisors and administrators minimize the problem, if they are not aware of the negative effects of burnout for staff, clients, and agencies, and if they do not realize the extent to which the structure of the work

> setting contributes to the problem, then little can be done to alleviate job stress and burnout in a setting (Cherniss, 1980b, p. 159).

Such awareness and attention need not cost a great deal nor take much time. For example, a manager who talks and listens to line and supervisory staff can gain at least some indication of problems.

A second point for managers to note is the dramatic relationship between job satisfaction and burnout. Some of the highest correlations in the data were between job satisfaction and burnout. At first blush, this may sound like another instance of social science demonstrating the obvious. As shown in Chapter 2, however, Maslach and Jackson (1981) specifically disclaimed a strong correlation between measures of the two concepts. Their contention, however, is not supported by the data on both the probation officers and the correctional officers. Furthermore, the relationship between job satisfaction and burnout suggests something to the correctional manager in terms of an intervention strategy. It says that whatever improves job satisfaction will also have an influence on burnout. Unlike the research on burnout, which is relatively recent, the research on job satisfaction has been conducted for decades. As noted in Chapter 6, one mid-1970s survey of the research on job satisfaction, for example, noted that more than 3,300 studies of job satisfaction had been conducted up to that point (Locke, 1976). Moreover, the satisfaction research has shown a pattern "beyond question" in terms of how jobs can be designed to satisfy and motivate workers:

> Both common sense and research answer these questions in terms of variety, complexity, autonomy, and responsibility. . . . Studies . . . show negative relations between external control of work pace and satisfaction. In fact the bulk of the research on satisfaction with jobs demonstrates that more varied, complex and challenging tasks are higher in worker gratification than less skilled routine jobs (Katz & Kahn, 1978, p. 364).

Thus, managers can utilize the plethora of job satisfaction information in the fight against burnout, confident that interventions suggested by such research will have some effect on burnout.

Managers also can benefit from another dramatic finding in the data: the lack of any direct or strong relationship between work load indicators and burnout. The implication is that simply reducing the work load will not necessarily prevent or reduce burnout; the problem is more complex. The strong relationship in the data between overload and burnout (see Chapter 6) suggests that it is more critical to ascertain the point at which work loads interfere with the individual worker's ability to get the job done than it is simply to reduce work loads. In accord with Cherniss (1980a, 1980b), the data suggest that probation workers want to be competent and effective. The data suggest that the critical question is not merely caseload size nor the simple number of investigations assigned an officer in a given month. Instead, the critical point is reached when a worker feels that there is so much to do that he cannot finish it or finish it well. One problem this poses, however, is that objectively unequal work loads may be subjectively equal. If a manager, therefore, attempts to take individual worker capability into consideration, he may face union opposition and/or worker resistance. Perhaps open discussion of the problem before implementation would prevent any such negative consequences. Also, the reward structure would have to be remodeled to fit any modifications in work assignments.

Managers, however, should not use the absence of a strong relationship between work load indicators and burnout to ignore the work demands they impose on employees. The importance of the overload variable points out that when workers perceive that they are overburdened burnout is more likely to occur. So it is important for managers to be aware of when individual workers are feeling overburdened. The subtle but important point of the research is that how a worker evaluates his or her workload is more critical in terms of burnout than any "objective" judgment about the worker's work load.

The findings also suggest that probation/parole managers and prison wardens pay special attention to the young and newly hired officers. Both the literature (Cherniss, 1980a, 1980b; Edelwich, 1980; Maslach, 1976) and the data here indicate that such workers start with positive attitudes toward their work. In a period of from six months to three years on the job, however, matters seem to deteriorate. Burnout appears to increase. Because this is survey rather than longitudinal research, it is more accurate to say that workers with increasing length of service (up to three years) reported increasing degrees of burnout. One concrete action that the data suggest would be effective is to initiate an orientation program, if one is not already in operation, or to improve the current program if examination reveals that it needs improvement. As Cherniss (1980b) has pointed out, an orientation program need not be elaborate and expensive to be effective. Even one- or two-day programs can have an effect. One effective program involved little more than a realistic orientation booklet. The booklet did not just inform new workers of fringe benefits but presented problems likely to occur and some proven methods for coping with such problems. The important point is that an effective orientation program can minimize the reality shock (Kramer, 1974) that many new workers, especially new graduates, face as they enter human service work.

The findings that probation workers with 15 years or more of experience and that older workers reported burnout levels about as low as neophyte officers should be encouraging news to these workers and to managers. In a society that has been youth oriented but now is becoming more and more concerned with the aging process, the findings are evidence of the positive contributions such employees can offer. Contrary to the stereotypes of some, these older, more experienced street-level bureaucrats are not automatically negative and uncaring. Perhaps as Blau (1974) suggested years ago, these workers have learned to manipulate some of the negative aspects of corrections to offer real service to individuals. One suggestion Cherniss (1980b) offers to take advantage of this adaptation is for an older worker, who is not the new employee's supervisor, to guide the new worker through the first few days of employment. In this way, the experienced worker can

share some of his/her coping skills with the new workers. Care is needed, of course, in assigning mentors who are not burned out themselves and who will not transmit negative coping skills (for a description of this, see McCleary, 1978, pp. 158–66).

The results also indicate that the perennial problem of the conflict between assistance and control is still present in probation/parole (63 percent of the respondents felt this to be so) and that it is related to burnout. As noted earlier and as discussed more fully later in this chapter, Thomson and Fogel (1980) argue that the Justice Model with its emphasis on the victim would so reorder probation as to sweep aside the conflict between assistance and control. In other words, Justice Model proponents contend that the conflict stems from too much preoccupation with the offender rather than concern for the offended. The pervasiveness of the problem, however, suggests that it cannot be resolved so simply. One approach for managers is to choose one emphasis or the other. Managers can follow Barkdull (1976) and call probation control and mean it, or they can follow Conrad (1973) in his call for the removal of all surveillance or law enforcement activities from probation and parole agencies. Another approach would be team approaches wherein individuals with an enforcement emphasis only monitor offenders and workers with an assistance orientation only counsel offenders or offer referral services (Dell'Apa et al., 1976). To some extent, the Georgia Intensive Probation Supervision program has adopted this suggestion; one officer is a surveillance officer who checks curfews and administers urinalyses, and the other member of the two-officer team is more of an assistance-oriented probation officer. But experience has shown that there is considerable "overlapping and even in some cases reversal of roles" (Erwin, 1987, p. 30) between the two, which also supports the pervasiveness of the problem.

The findings also indicate that intersender role conflict — the problem of conflicting expectations — is related to burnout. This more abstract problem may refer to conflicting expectations for assistance versus control or may refer to any conflicting expectations. The implication for managers is to look for the presence of such conflicting expectations in their agencies. Do supervisors want comprehensive presentence investigations whereas judges read only the recommendation or the evaluative summary at the end of the report? Do supervisors emphasize paperwork while officers want to engage in client contact? Do state administrators stress accountability and red tape while line workers want to take legitimate risks? The findings on role conflict suggest that managers consider these and other possible manifestations of incompatible demands being placed on correctional employees, whatever the source.

Although not included in the multivariate analysis, two items noted in Chapter 8 (see Table 8.3) deserve comment here. The probation officers were overwhelmingly in agreement about two "bread-and-butter" issues: pay satisfaction and satisfaction with the degree of promotional opportunities. Only 25 percent of the line officers were satisfied with their pay, and only 5 percent were satisfied with the degree of promotional opportunities in the field. In contrast, in *The 1977 Quality of Employment Survey* 73 percent of the respondents (from various occupations) agreed that their pay was "good," and 48 percent felt that their chances for promotion were "good" (Quinn & Staines, 1979, pp. 217 & 219). Despite some differences in item wording, these contrasts are dramatic; probation officers reported faring worse than workers in many other types of work. Given shrinking governmental budgets, it is unrealistic to expect pay raises or job upgradings in response to worker dissatisfaction. At the same time, one has to wonder about the realism of localities that pay abysmally low salaries. Similarly, one wonders about the rationality of a civil service system in which an officer achieves tenure in one year and reaches maximum pay, except for token longevity increases, after five years of service. Often, the only way to achieve higher pay and to achieve a promotion is to leave offender service work for a managerial position. The research reported here and elsewhere (e.g., Polisky, 1981b) shows that probation/parole officers want opportunities for advancement. One possible solution is to establish a career ladder in which one can move from apprentice, to officer, to senior or master officer. In that way, an individual can achieve both prestige and higher pay without relinquishing line work for undesired managerial responsibilities. At the very least, what needs to be avoided is any "self-defeating personnel system" involving either "favoritism, cronyism, and arbitrariness" or "paper-pencil testing irrationality" (Clear, 1985, p. 41). In summary, the findings here do not delineate a solution, but they clearly demonstrate that pay and the degree of promotional opportunities available are two problem areas in correctional employment.

Concerning the latter problem of the lack of promotional opportunities or career ladders in probation and parole, Cherniss (1980b) has noted that this is a problem in human service work in general. He offers some job enrichment suggestions that might be practical in corrections. First, staff in a program for troubled adolescents were encouraged to develop their own evening programs, such as group counseling, karate, or woodworking. This allowed staff "to experience the joy of creating in a way that was not possible in any other part of their job" (Cherniss, 1980b, p. 170). Cherniss also found that allowing staff to engage in research allows them to satisfy some growth needs not met in their primary responsibilities. This research does not have to be an elaborate, statistical study, but could be description and analysis of difficult cases. Such a research effort had positive benefits in one mental health program:

> Because research and education were major goals in this program, staff were given time to think about, discuss, and write about particularly illuminating cases. The insights that came from this endeavor were communicated to practitioners in other programs through articles, workshops, and conferences. Not only was this type of research absorbing and interesting, it also provided new opportunities for recognition and accomplishment (Cherniss, 1980b, p. 182).

Although McCleary (1978) was quite negative in his assessment of the motivational potential of parole officers (he classified all the officers as lazy, Theory X individuals), he did report that a significant number of the officers, on their own initiative, organized group counseling sessions for parolees. This indicates that many officers may devote considerable energy to creative and innovative job-related pursuits if given the chance. The overall point is that administrators should consider ways to allow staff members to keep growing professionally even in the face of budgets that may make pay raises or career ladders elusive goals.

Implications for Line Workers

At the level of the individual officer, awareness also seems to be a logical first course of action. Perhaps even as recently as five years ago workers could enter probation, parole, or prison work unaware of the inherent difficulties. Given the writing on reality shock (Kramer, 1974), burnout (Cherniss, 1980a, 1980b; Maslach, 1982), probation officers (Brown 1986, 1987), parole officers (McCleary, 1978; Studt, 1973), and correctional officers (e.g., Johnson, 1987; Philiber, 1987), however, it is becoming almost impossible to enter the field without an awareness of the problems. Thus, even if deficient college programs or deficient orientation programs ignore problems, individual workers can read about them, attend workshops, and perhaps even help to raise consciousness levels at the workplace.

As mentioned earlier, exercise did not emerge as the potent medicine that some (e.g., Freudenberger, 1974; Yates, 1979) suggested it would. But the data did not suggest that exercise intensifies burnout. {erhaps item construction error or some other problem masked the true importance of exercise in this research. The most cautious conclusion from the data at hand is simply that the findings neither confirmed nor denied the hypothesized relationship between exercise and burnout. In congruence with this, a stress reduction experiment in Michigan found that although police officers involved in an exercise program "showed some improvement as a result of their participation in the experiment, they also demonstrated some deterioration" (O'Neill et al., 1981).

Similar ambivalence is true for other factors over which the individual has control. Variables such as marital status, religiosity, number of children in one's care, the presence of supportive friends at work, and how frequently one lunches with coworkers all emerged as less than meaningful inhibitors of burnout. As was the case with the exercise variable, however, there is no dramatic evidence that these factors intensify burnout. Thus, this research fails to offer any dramatic evidence that these variables, which can be used as indices of support, either inhibit or intensify the experience of burnout.

Perhaps the failure of most of these individual level variables to show strong relationships to burnout is indirect evidence for Cherniss's contention that organizational factors are of more importance in understanding burnout and in attempting any intervention: "It is easier to restructure a role than to restructure the character of either an individual or a society" (Cherniss, 1980b, p. 158). The importance of organizational factors in understanding and improving worker job attitudes is far from new (see, e.g., Perrow, 1970). Thus, both Cherniss and the data suggest that the individual try to improve the situation at work rather than focus on individual factors at work or outside work.

Implications for Mission Reform

Recent writing on probation has not always been kind. A mid-1970s study by the General Accounting Office (1976) indicated that many officers were simply not doing their jobs. Specifically, that report found that 60 percent of the conditions of probation were not enforced and that 60 percent of the probation case records studied did not even have written case plans. An investigation of juvenile probation in New York City (McFadden, 1982) found that many officers were sitting idle while complaining of high caseloads. A study of felony probationers in California found that two-thirds were rearrested within 40 months (Petersilia et al., 1985). A recent study of juveniles in probation in Utah indicated that notification probation — being on probation without any supervision by an officer — was just as effective as regular *and* intensive supervision (National Council on Crime and Delinquency, 1987).

Other reports, however, have been more positive. A study of felony probationers in Kentucky (Vito, 1986), for example, indicated that the recidivism rate was considerably lower than that found in California. Similarly, the Utah study of juvenile probation (National Council on Crime and Delinquency, 1987) indicated support for probation over institutionalization. Available evidence on an intensive probation supervision program in Georgia (Erwin, 1986, 1987) indicates that it is a viable alternative to incarceration for select categories of felons. Finally, evidence is still being collected on innovations in probation such as house arrest and electronic monitoring of probationers (see, e.g., Petersilia, 1986; Schmidt, 1986).

Nevertheless, the negative reports on the health of probation have raised profound questions about the mission of probation. Experts, system personnel, and concerned citizens alike have been questioning the purpose of probation (see, e.g., Thomson, 1987). What used to be taken for granted is now in dispute.

Here the question arises whether reconsideration of the community correctional mission might also improve the field as an occupation. Can any change in mission also improve the conditions of the workers? Specifically, can any such change assist the workers in their search for a sense of efficacy? It is important to review recent proposals to improve probation and parole to see if these proposals might also inhibit burnout or exacerbate it.

Perhaps the most idealistic proposal is the Justice Model of probation in which punishment, proportionality, consideration for victims, restitution, and community service take key places (Fogel, McAnany, & Thomson, 1980; McAnany, Thomson, & Fogel, 1984). Justice Model adherents suggest that probation be transformed from leniency to fair and proportional punishment via such mechanisms as frequent reporting by probationers, restitution orders wherever appropriate, and community service requirements. Thus, probation would clearly entail "a restriction of liberty" (Fogel, McAnany, & Thomson,

1980, p. 7), and the probation officer's role would change from therapist to that of monitor of compliance with the conditions of the court order of probation:

> The probation officer is thus neither a cop nor a counselor; he/she is an officer of the court. As such, he/she is responsible for monitoring compliance with the demands of justice, but at the same time is permitted, even encouraged, to aid the probationer in ways in which the probationer would like to be aided and in which the officer is competent to provide aid. In effect, the probation officer is the representative of the court in ensuring that the sentence of probation is carried out, and at a more abstract level, that justice is served (Thomson & Fogel, 1980, pp. 13–14).

In this perspective, probation would have multiple roles and officers could generalize — engage in all the roles — or engage in a specific role. The roles would include that of mediator between offenders and victims, monitor of offender compliance with court orders, and service broker to offenders. According to the theorists, the conflict between assistance and control would be avoided because there would be no nexus between assistance and any promise of leniency.

The critical question in terms of burnout considerations is whether the Justice Model would alter the occupation so as to prevent burnout. At least there is provision for a variety of roles, contrary to some of the models discussed below that offer a very narrow role — report writer — for officers. In contrast to the present (recent) rehabilitation or casework model, the Justice Model offers more clearly defined roles: rather than vague exhortations to assist or rehabilitate, Justice Model theorists suggest specific tasks such as the determination of restitution, the monitoring of compliance with court orders, and the referral of offenders to community services in order to assist them in such compliance. Both the literature on job satisfaction (Katz & Kahn, 1978) and burnout (Cherniss, 1980b) suggest that such variety and clearly defined roles (versus role ambiguity) would be positive features of jobs rather than causes of dissatisfaction and burnout. Likewise, Justice Model theorists contend that the focus on the role of monitor would transcend the perennial problem of role conflict between an emphasis on assistance and an emphasis on control for officers.

Some questions remain, however, whether probation officers would fare better under the Justice Model than under other proposals. Perhaps the main question is whether the Justice Model would allow officers opportunities to achieve high levels of both intrinsic job satisfaction and personal accomplishment. Recall from Chapter 5 that many officers reported positive levels of these two variables. A valid question is whether officers would indeed react favorably to the more limited, although more clearly delineated, probation officer role offered by the Justice Model. More specific questions concern such matters as the suggestion of Justice Model theorists that some probationers report everyday. Such conditions sound beneficial but degenerate in practice because judges are reluctant to enforce them; very few judges are willing to revoke probation and return someone to jail for missing one or two trips a week to the probation office. Offenders learn very quickly that they can skip one or two reports a week without reprisal.

Quite similar to the Justice Model is Galaway's (1983) proposal that probation become a reparative sentence. Like the Justice Model theorists, Galaway proposes the utilization of both restitution to victims and community service. In addition, he suggests that each probationer have a community sponsor whose duties would be "to provide support and encouragement to the offender and to assist the probation office in overseeing completion of the reparative sentence requirements" (Galaway, 1983, p. 10). All of this is directed at the lofty goal of "reconciliation of the offender to the community" (Galaway, 1983, p. 15). Because the reparative sentence model is essentially the same as the Justice Model, its implications for the work lives of probation officers are essentially the same.

At the other end of the spectrum is the pessimistic conclusion of Rosecrance (1986) that probation supervision is an impossible mission and should be eliminated:

> Such an action would relieve probation officers of the control-assistance dilemma and free them to concentrate upon supplying objective and accurate information to the court. Probation departments would be charged with the responsibility of compiling and presenting court evaluations. If probation is recommended and counseling or treatment is needed, they would be provided by agencies outside the criminal justice system. Monitoring those placed on probation would become a computerized function performed by clerical employees of the court. With this type of reorganization probation would have a parsimonious and achievable mission — providing indepth court investigation services (Rosecrance, 1986, p. 26).

Several comments are in order. First, this seemingly radical suggestion is not entirely novel. Conrad (1973) made essentially the same suggestion more than a decade ago when he suggested that probation be divided into two distinct functions: offender referral for services and the collection of information for the courts. That is, he suggested that some workers now called probation or parole officers be assigned to become referral agents or brokers who would assist offenders in finding appropriate services such as employment agencies. Other current probation officers would be called information officers and specialize in presentence reports. Rather than suggesting that monitoring of offender compliance with court conditions be accomplished by computers and clerical personnel, however, Conrad suggested that law enforcement functions of probation be relegated to the police "who are trained for the task and organized to do it" (Conrad, 1973, p. 216). Conrad (1984) recently restated his proposal in a book on the Justice Model in probation (McAnany, Thomson, & Fogel, 1984).

A second comment on Rosecrance's (1986) proposal is an expression of concern whether his proposed role for probation officers, providing information to the courts, is broad enough to satisfy most officers. Univariate analysis of the data on probation officers in Connecticut, Indiana, and New York showed no differences in burnout scores for generalists compared to specialists. In a more detailed analysis, however, officers who specialized in investigations reported the worst emotional exhaustion and personal accomplishment scores. These findings were weak, but they suggest that the role of investigator or court information officer might be problematic. Referring to human service work in general, rather than probation in particular, Cherniss (1980b) took the position that a generalist role with a variety of tasks involved in the role is less conducive to burnout than a specialist role. Thus, he would appear to be opposed to the proposal of either Rosecrance or Conrad for radical specialization in probation. On the positive side, either proposal would eliminate role conflict (any conflict between assistance and control) and role ambiguity. The question is whether they would also eliminate many satisfying aspects of the job that allow workers to feel that they are making some changes in the lives of others.

Somewhere in between the idealism of the Justice and reparative sentence models and the pessimism-realism of Rosecrance and Conrad is the suggestion of O'Leary and Clear (1984) that probation and parole assume the mission of risk control. This is a utilitarian model incorporating concern for both fair punishment and offender risk. The former seeks retribution and deterrence; the latter seeks incapacitative ends. The emphasis on fair punishment sets limits on any sentence; the emphasis on control of offender risk allows variation within such limits according to prediction of risk potential.

In the risk control model, many of the conditions of probation would be preventive conditions "employed only when there is substantial reason to believe that [their] imposition is immediately, directly, and importantly related to the ability of an offender to conform to a punitive condition and/or to reside satisfactorily in the community without committing serious crime" (O'Leary & Clear, 1984, p. 18). Assistance actions on the part of the officer would be appropriate only if related to crime control objectives or, if not related to crime control objectives, only if mutually agreed upon by officer and probationer. Other than the emphasis on prediction, crime control, and limited assistance to probationers, the role of the officer is very similar to that proposed in the Justice Model — "to make certain that the conditions laid down by the court or parole board are observed" (O'Leary & Clear, 1984, p. 18).

Because this model offers more variety than the Justice, reparative, or Rosecrance models, it appears to be more positive in its implications for officers. Officers would be concerned with such things as monitoring offender compliance with court conditions, but they would also have the very important tasks of attempting to predict risk potential and trying to assist probationers/parolees to live in accordance with the conditions of their probation/parole orders. At least on the surface the assistance-control dilemma is resolved; officers could enforce assistance-oriented requirements only if they were related to punitive or risk control conditions. Officers could not just insist that an offender get counseling or enroll in an educational program simply because the officer "felt it was good" for the offender. Such variety and such restriction, but not elimination, of the assistance role would appear to have positive possibilities for improved working conditions and less burnout.

Probably the biggest problem with the model is its emphasis on risk control, prediction, and incapacitation. All of this translates into discretion, which proved to be a stumbling block and point of contention in past probation and parole efforts. O'Leary and Clear (1984) are convinced that such discretion can be controlled rather than abused and that it can be based on research evidence rather than on whim and caprice. Only implementation of their model will reveal whether the critics of incapacitation (e.g., von Hirsch, 1984) or the proponents (e.g., O'Leary & Clear, 1984; Greenwood, 1984) are right.

Another model for probation/parole is what Fogel (1984) calls a needs provision model and what Rosecrance (1986) calls a service orientation. In this model, community corrections should focus on assisting offenders in resolving their problems; problem resolution, in turn, will mean that offenders will no longer have the deficits or needs that led them to turn to crime. This model casts probation/parole officers as direct service providers or as brokers and advocates of offenders to community services. Calls for direct service provision — officers as counselors and job finders — are seen frequently in perhaps the leading grass-roots probation journal, *Federal Probation* (e.g., Assur, Jackson, & Muncy, 1987; Dierna, 1987; Van Deusen, Yarbrough, & Cornelsen, 1985; Wooten, 1985). Many have also called for a broker, advocate, or case manager role (Dietrich, 1979) for the officer. In either form, the focus is on helping the offender, with the presence of some modicum of a law enforcement function; offenders who break the rules and refuse assistance are returned to court or to prison.

Arguably, many, if not most, of the officers surveyed in this report fit into this service orientation, if only by default. The officers in Connecticut, Indiana, and New York were surveyed in 1981, before much of the theorizing on mission reform noted in this chapter. The officers in Alabama were surveyed in 1984, before the speculation had run its full course. Thus, it can be argued that probation or parole focused on service orientation or needs provision is rife with the possibility of the burnout problems reported in this study. More specifically, it is likely that a significant minority of the officers in such agencies will report emotional exhaustion, depersonalization, and lack of personal accomplishment.

Implications for Future Research

This research suggests several avenues for future research. First, it is clear that burnout is a problem for a significant minority of correctional employees and deserves further research attention. Although the problem does not appear to be of epidemic proportions, that burnout was found in workers in several states demonstrates the importance of the problem. Thus, future research is warranted. Such research should seek refinement of knowledge about the extent and causes of the problem and about effective prevention and intervention techniques. This research should include sophisticated survey research, longitudinal, and, if possible, experimental designs. For example, perhaps interventions can be tested on experimental groups versus control groups to determine their differential effectiveness. Similarly, cohorts of workers can be followed from initial hiring and orientation to early adjustment on the job, where burnout is very possible, to either termination, stagnation, or positive coping.

One technical question that needs to be addressed is whether personal accomplishment is indeed distinct from intrinsic job satisfaction. As Chapter 5 indicated, this research found considerable overlap between Maslach and Jackson's (1981) measure of accomplishment and a measure of intrinsic job satisfaction. If the Maslach Burnout Inventory (now called the Human Services Survey) is to continue as a standard measure of burnout, this issue needs clear resolution.

A very practical research strategy at this point in the history of corrections would be to analyze the experiences of workers in several of the intensive supervision efforts currently under way. Now is the time for quasi-experimental designs comparing correctional workers in traditional assignments with workers in innovative, recently devised intensive supervision programs such as those being conducted in Alabama, Georgia, New Jersey, and New York (see, e.g., McCarthy, 1987 for a discussion of such programs). Similarly, workers in house arrest and electronic monitoring programs can be tracked to see if burnout develops. Many of these efforts are under scrutiny to see if their recidivism rates are lower than past reforms; from the worker's standpoint, it is also important that they be tracked in terms of their effects on such worker concerns as job satisfaction, job stress, and burnout. Such concerns seem particularly appropriate given the high expectations and demands being placed on many of the workers in such programs. When the author and a colleague conducted research on Alabama's Supervised Intensive Restitution program, for example, program officers were expected to report to work at 7 a.m. to make sure that offenders assigned to community service work projects were present and working. After working a regular day, these same officers were also expected to make night curfew checks after 10 p.m. and weekend checks. Although initial research and a one-year followup (Lindquist & Whitehead, 1986a, 1986b, 1986c; Whitehead & Lindquist, 1987) indicated that the officers were very positive about their jobs and were reporting lower burnout scores than both regular prison guards and regular parole officers, such dedication and positive adjustment can be maintained only so long. As Conrad (1987, p. 63) has noted, "Any program that is based on constructive personal relations must be carried out by normal people — not by saintly deviates who neither have nor want private lives of their own." Now that these intensive supervision programs have existed for a few years, it is important to determine the long-term effects on the workers as well as on recidivism rates. Unfortunately, past experience indicates that concern for the workers is often a low priority.

This is both unfortunate and unwise. A clear message from past research on corrections, in particular (e.g., McCleary, 1978; Waller, 1974), and on human service workers, in general (Blau, 1974; Lipsky, 1980), is that line officers are the ones who, for better or worse, implement policy. Any mission reform in probation, parole, or prisons is ultimately implemented and shaped by the probation, parole, or correctional officer who actually interacts with inmates. Both academic and executive suggestions are only as good as the officer who follows them. Thus, inattention to the needs of line workers is both shortsighted and fatal. Without the worker, corrections is a set of ideals and promises; with the worker, corrections becomes reality.

The final implication for future research is a call for a broader focus. Although concern about burnout is important and should not be ignored, research attention should also be focused on those who cope in a positive way and do not burn out. Because they do not cause managers or clients any problems, workers who cope often are neglected. This is unfortunate for two reasons. First, analysis of these workers can offer insights to those who are not coping. Second, attention to the workers who are doing well can benefit the organization and the clientele. As noted previously, even the late critic of correctional effectiveness, Robert Martinson (1974), conceded that effective correctional programs depended on offender "contact with one of the 'good people' who are frequently in such short supply" (p. 46). In other words, productive workers can make a difference in offenders' lives, and such results reflect favorably on the organization.

At least part of any future research, therefore, should focus on productive and positive workers. Like research on private corporations (see, e.g., Peters & Waterman, 1982; Peters, 1985), correctional research needs to look at both excellent individuals and excellent organizations. Too often the probation, parole, and prison literature has focused only on the problems. Those problems are there, and they need to be addressed. Successes are also there, however, and they too need to be addressed so that other correctional workers and organizations can benefit from their success. What future researchers must do, therefore, is to devote attention to the positive and productive workers as well as to those workers experiencing problems. It is hoped that such a balanced approach will result in strategies to help successful workers continue and to help other workers overcome problems so that they too can be positive and productive.

References

Adler, F., with Adler, H. M. (1975). *Sisters in crime.* New York: McGraw-Hill.

Allen, H. E., Eskridge, C. W., Latessa, E. J., & Vito, G. F. (1985). *Probation and parole in America.* New York: Macmillan.

American Correctional Association (1981). *Probation and parole directory.* College Park, MD: Author.

Asher, H. B. (1983). *Causal modeling.* Beverly Hills, CA: Sage.

Assur, E. R., Jackson, G. W., & Muncy, T. (1987). Probation counselors and the adult children of alcoholics. *Federal Probation, 51* (3), 41–46.

Babbie, E. (1986). *The practice of social research* (4th ed.). Belmont, CA: Wadsworth.

Ball, R. A., & Lilly, J. R. (1986). A theoretical examination of home incarceration. *Federal Probation, 50* (1), 17–24.

Barad, C. B. (1979). *Study of burnout syndrome among Social Security Administration field public contact employees.* Unpublished report, Social Security Administration.

Barkdull, W. L. (1976). Probation: Call it control — and mean it. *Federal Probation, 40* (4), 3–8.

Bartollas, C. (1981). *Introduction to corrections.* New York: Harper & Row.

Beck, D. F. (1987). Counselor burnout in family service agencies. *Social Casework, 68,* 3–15.

Belcastro, P. A., Gold, R. S., & Grant, J. (1982). Stress and burnout: Physiologic effects on correctional teachers. *Criminal Justice and Behavior, 9,* 387–95.

Bernhard, M. (1981, May 10). Helping others takes a toll: Clergy burnout. Albany (NY) *Times Union,* p. A-3.

Blau, P. (1974). *On the nature of organizations.* New York: Wiley.

Blostein, S., Eldridge, W., Kilty, K., & Richardson, V. (1985). A multidimensional analysis of the concept of burnout. *Employee Assistance Quarterly, 1* (2), 55–66.

Blough, S. G. (1980). Perceived stress as a function of setting and personality (Doctoral dissertation, The Ohio State University, 1980). *Dissertation Abstracts International, 41,* 4285.

Blumberg, A. S. (1979). *Criminal justice: Issues and ironies* (2d ed.). New York: New Viewpoints.

Blumberg, P. (1976). *Industrial democracy: The sociology of participation.* New York: Schocken.

Bowker, L. H. (1982). *Corrections: The science and the art.* New York: Macmillan.

Bradley, H. B. (1969). Community-based treatment for young adult offenders. *Crime and Delinquency, 15,* 359–70.

Brennan, W. C., & Khinduka, S. K. (1970). Role discrepancies and professional socialization: The case of the juvenile probation officer. *Social Work, 15,* 87–94.

Bridgwater, C. A. (1984, May). Hill Street burnout blues. *Psychology Today,* p. 70.

Brief, A., Munro, J., & Aldag, R. (1976). Correctional employees' reactions to job characteristics: A data based argument for job enlargement. *Journal of Criminal Justice, 4,* 223–30.

Brief, A. P., Schuler, R. S., & Van Sell, M. (1981). *Managing job stress.* Boston: Little, Brown.

Brown, P. W. (1986). Probation officer burnout: An organizational disease/an organizational cure. *Federal Probation, 50* (1), 4–7.

Brown, P. W. (1987). Probation officer burnout: An organizational disease/an organizational cure. Part II. *Federal Probation, 51* (3), 17–21.

Burke, R. J., & Deszca, E. (1986). Correlates of psychological burnout phases among police officers. *Human Relations, 39,* 487–502.

Burke, R. J., Shearer, J., & Deszca, E. (1984). Burnout among men and women in police work: An examination of the Cherniss model. *Journal of Health and Human Resources Administration, 7,* 162–88.

Burke, R. J., & Weir, T. (1980). Coping with the stress of managerial occupations. In C. L. Cooper & R. Payne (eds.), *Current concerns in occupational stress* (pp. 299–335). New York: Wiley.

Byrne, J. M. (1986). The control controversy: A preliminary examination of intensive probation supervision programs in the United States. *Federal Probation, 50* (2), 4–16.

Caplan, R. D. (1985). Psychosocial stress in work. *Management and Labour Studies, 10* (2), 63–76.

Carter, R. M., Glaser, D., & Wilkins, L. T. (1976). Caseloads: Some conceptual models. In R. M. Carter & L. T. Wilkins (eds.), *Probation, parole, and community corrections* (2d ed.) (pp. 381–401). New York: John Wiley.

____. (1984). *Probation, parole, and community corrections* (3rd ed.). New York: John Wiley.

Cheek, F., & Miller, M. (1983). The experience of stress for corrections officers. *Journal of Criminal Justice, 11,* 105–20.

Cherniss, C. (1980a). *Professional burnout in human service organizations.* New York: Praeger.

____. (1980b). *Staff burnout: Job stress in the human services.* Beverly Hills, CA: Sage.

____. (1985). Stress, burnout, and the special services provider. *Special Services in the Schools, 2,* 45–61.

Cherniss, C., & Egnatios, E. (1978). Clinical Supervision in community mental health work. *Social Work, 23,* 219–33.

Chesney, M. A., & Roseman, R. H. (1980). Type A behaviour in the work setting. In C. L. Cooper & R. Payne (eds.), *Current concerns in occupational stress* (pp. 187–212). New York: Wiley.

Cjapo, M., & Clarke, R. (1976). Probation officers for juveniles in Canada. *Canadian Journal of Criminology, 18,* 290–301.

Clarke, S. H. (1979). What is the purpose of probation and why do we revoke it? *Crime and Delinquency, 25,* 409–24.

Clear, T. R. (1985). Managerial issues in community corrections. In L. F. Travis (ed.), *Probation, parole, and community corrections: A reader* (pp. 33–46). Prospect Heights, IL: Waveland.

Clear, T. R., & O'Leary, V. (1983). *Controlling the offender in the community.* Lexington, MA: Lexington.

Cleary, P., & Mechanic, D. (1983). Sex differences in psychological distress among married people. *Journal of Health and Social Behavior, 24,* 111–21.

Conrad, J. P. (1973). Corrections and simple justice. *Journal of Criminal Law and Criminology, 64,* 208–17.

____. (1982). Can corrections be rehabilitated? *Federal Probation, 46* (2), 3–8.

____. (1984). The redefinition of probation: Drastic proposals to solve an urgent problem. In P. D. McAnany, D. Thomson, and D. Fogel (eds.), *Probation and justice: Reconsideration of mission* (pp. 251–73).

____. (1987). News of the future: The intensive revolution. *Federal Probation, 51* (2), 62–64.

Cope, D. (1979). Understanding the concept of job satisfaction. In R. G. Sell & P. Shipley, *Satisfactions in work design: Ergonomics and other approaches.* London: Taylor & Francis.

Crouch, B. M., & Alpert, G. P. (1982). Sex and occupational socialization among prison guards: A longitudinal study. *Criminal Justice and Behavior, 9,* 159–76.

Cullen, F. T., & Gilbert, K. E. (1982). *Reaffirming rehabilitation.* Cincinnati: Anderson.

Cullen, F. T., Link, B. G., Travis, L. F., & Lemming, T. (1983). Paradox in policing: A note on perceptions of danger. *Journal of Police Science and Administration, 11,* 457–62.

Cullen, F. T., Link, B. G., Wolfe, N. T., & Frank, J. (1985). The social dimensions of correctional officer stress. *Justice Quarterly, 4,* 505–33.

Czajkoski, E. H. (1969). Functional specialization in probation and parole. *Crime and Delinquency, 15,* 227–37.

Dahl, J. J. (1979). *Management of stress in corrections.* Washington, D.C.: U.S. Department of Justice.

Daley, M. R. (1979). "Burnout:" Smoldering problem in protective services. *Social Work, 5,* 375–79.

Dell'Apa, F., Adams, W. T., Jorgensen, J. D., & Sigurdson, H. R. (1976). Advocacy, brokerage, community: The abc's of probation and parole. *Federal Probation, 40* (4), 37–44.

Dierna, J. S. (1987). Counseling in federal probation: The introduction of a flowchart into the counseling process. *Federal Probation, 51* (3), 4–16.

Dietrich, S. G. (1979). The probation officer as therapist. *Federal Probation, 43* (2), 14–19.

Dignam, J. T., Barrera, M., & West, S. G. (1986). Occupational stress, social support, and burnout among correctional officers. *American Journal of Community Psychology, 14,* 177–93.

Duffee, D. (1980). *Correctional management: Change and control in correctional organizations.* Englewood Cliffs, NJ: Prentice-Hall.

Edelwich, J., with Brodsky, A. (1980). *Burnout: Stages of disillusionment in the helping professions.* New York: Human Services Press.

Eliot, R., & Bred, D. (1984). *Is it worth dying for? A self-assessment program to make stress work for you, not against you.* New York: Bantam Books.

Erickson, C. L. (1977). Faking it: Principles of expediency as applied to probation. *Federal Probation, 41* (3), 36–39.

____. (1978). A p.o.'s lament: Have you ever had one of those days? *Federal Probation, 42* (3), 23–25.

____. (1980). *The perils of probation.* Springfield, IL: Charles C. Thomas.

Erwin, B. S. (1987). *Evaluation of intensive probation supervision in Georgia: Final report.* Atlanta: Georgia Department of Corrections.

____. (1986). Turning up the heat on probationers in Georgia. *Federal Probation, 50* (2), 17–24.

Etheridge, R., Hale, C., & Hambrick, M. (1984). Female employees in all-male correctional facilities. *Federal Probation, 48* (4), 54–65.

Etzion, D., & Pines, A. (1986). Sex and culture in burnout and coping among human service professionals: A social psychological perspective. *Journal of Cross-Cultural Psychology, 17,* 191–209.

Farmer, R. (1977). Cynicism: A factor in corrections work. *Journal of Criminal Justice, 5,* 237–46.

Festinger, L. (1957). *A theory of cognitive dissonance.* Evanston, IL: Row, Peterson.

Flowers, R. (1987). *Women and criminality: The woman as victim, offender, and practitioner.* New York: Greenwood Press.

Fogel, D. (1984). The emergence of probation as a profession in the service of public safety: The next ten years. In P. D. McAnany, D. Thomson, and D. Fogel (eds.), *Probation and justice: Reconsideration of mission* (pp. 65–99). Cambridge, MA: Oelgeschlager, Gunn, & Hain.

Fogel, D., McAnany, P. D., & Thomson, D. (1980). Probation as the pursuit of justice. Paper presented at the International Seminar on Community Corrections, Niagara Falls, NY.

Frazier, C. E., Bock, W. E., & Henretta, J. C. (1983). The role of probation officers in determining gender differences in sentencing severity. *Sociological Quarterly, 24,* 305–18.

Freudenberger, H. (1974). Staff burnout. *Journal of Social Issues, 30,* 159–65.

____. (1980). *Burn-out: The high cost of high achievement.* Garden City, NY: Anchor Press.

____. (1986). The issues of staff burnout in therapeutic communities. *Journal of Psychoactive Drugs, 18,* 247–51.

Friedman, M. & Ulmer, D. (1984). *Treating type A behavior — and your heart.* New York: Knopf.

Fry, L. W., & Greenfeld, S. (1980). An examination of attitudinal differences between policewomen and policemen. *Journal of Applied Psychology, 65,* 123–26.

Galaway, B. (1983). Probation: A reparative sentence. *Federal Probation, 47,* 9–15.

General Accounting Office. (1976). *State and county probation systems in crisis.* Washington, D.C.: U.S. Government Printing Office.

Gilsinan, J. F. (1982). *Doing justice: How the system works — as seen by the participants.* Englewood Cliffs, NJ: Prentice-Hall.

Glaser, D. (1969). *The effectiveness of a prison and parole system.* Indianapolis: Bobbs-Merrill.

Golden, K. M. (1982). Women in criminal justice: Occupational interests. *Journal of Criminal Justice, 10,* 147–52.

Golembiewski, R. T., & Munzenrider, R. F. (1984). Phases of psychological burn-out and organizational covariants: A replication using norms from a large population. *Journal of Health and Human Resources Administration, 7,* 290–323.

Golembiewski, R. T., Munzenrider, R. F., & Carter, D. (1983). Phases of progressive burnout and their work site covariants: Critical issues in organization development research and praxis. *Journal of Applied Behavioral Science, 19,* 461–82.

Golembiewski, R. T., Munzenrider, R. F., & Stevenson, J. G. (1986). *Stress in organizations: Toward a phase model of burnout.* New York: Praeger.

Golembiewski, R. T., & Roundtree, B. H. (1986, Summer). Phases of burn-out and properties of work environments: Replicating and extending a pattern of covariants. *Organization Development Journal,* 25–30.

Gore, S., & Mangione, T. W. (1983). Social roles, sex roles, and psychological distress: Additive and interactive models of sex differences. *Journal of Health and Social Behavior, 24,* 300–12.

Gorsuch, R. L. (1974). *Factor analysis.* Philadelphia: W. B. Saunders.

Graf, F. A. (1986). The relationship between social support and occupational stress among police officers. *Journal of Police Science and Administration, 14,* 178–86.

Gray, R. (1986). Probation: An exploration in meaning. *Federal Probation, 50* (4), 26–31.

Greenwood, P. W. (1984, January). Selective incapacitation: A method of using our prisons more effectively. *National Institute of Justice Reports,* pp. 4–7.

Guralnik, D. B. (ed.) (1980). *Webster's new world dictionary of the American language* (2d college ed.). New York: Simon & Schuster.

Hackman, J. R., & Oldham, G. R. (1974). The Job Diagnostic Survey: An instrument for the diagnosis of jobs and the evaluation of job redesign projects. *JSAS Catalog of Selected Documents in Psychology, 4,* 148 (Ms. No. 810).

Hagan, J. (1975). The social and legal construction of criminal justice. *Social Problems, 22,* 620–37.

Harrison, W. D. (1980). Role strain and burnout in child-protective service workers. *Social Services Review, 54,* 31–44.

Haw, M. A. (1982). Women, work and stress: A review and agenda for the future. *Journal of Health and Social Behavior, 23,* 132–44.

Hernandez, E. (1982). Females in law enforcement: Femininity, competence, attraction, and work acceptance. *Criminal Justice and Behavior, 9,* 13–34.

Herzberg, F. (1976). *The managerial choice: To be efficient and to be human.* Homewood, IL: Dow Jones-Irwin.

Hulin, C., & Blood, M. (1968). Job enlargement, individual differences, and worker responses. *Psychological Bulletin, 69,* 41–55.

Hussey, F. A., & Duffee, D. E. (1980). *Probation, parole, and community field services: Policy, structure, and process.* New York: Harper & Row.

Indiana Judicial Conference. (1982). *Probation officer's handbook.* Indianapolis: Author.

Irwin, J. (1970). *The felon.* Englewood Cliffs, NJ: Prentice-Hall.

Iwanicki, E. F., & Schwab, R. L. (1981). A cross validation study of the Maslach Burnout Inventory. *Educational and Psychological Measurement, 41,* 1167–74.

Jackson, S. E., Schuler, R. S., & Schwab, R. L. (1986). Toward an understanding of the burnout phenomenon. *Journal of Applied Psychology, 71,* 630–40.

Jacobs, J. B. (1978). What prison guards think: A profile of the Illinois force. *Crime and Delinquency, 24,* 185–96.

Jacobs, J. B., & Kraft, L. (1978). Integrating the keepers: A comparison of black and white prison guards. *Social Problems, 25,* 304–18.

Jayewardene, C. H. S., & D. J. N. Jayasuriya (1981). *The management of correctional institutions.* Toronto: Butterworths.

Johnson, R. (1977). Ameliorating prison stress: Some helping roles for custodial personnel. *International Journal of Criminology and Penology, 5,* 263–73.

____. (1987). *Hard time: Understanding and reforming the prison.* Monterey, CA: Brooks/Cole.

Johnson, W. (1984, April). Career burnout. *Essence,* p. 24.

Kahn, R. L. (1978). Job burnout: prevention and remedies. *Public Welfare, 36,* 61–63.

Kahn, R. L., Wolfe, D. M., Quinn, R. P., Snoek, J. D., & Rosenthal, R. A. (1964). *Organizational stress: Studies in role conflict and ambiguity.* New York: Wiley.

Karger, H. J. (1981). Burnout as alienation. *Social Service Review, 55,* 270–83.

Karlinsky, S. (1979). Job satisfaction among living unit and nonliving unit staff in a Canadian penitentiary. Unpublished doctoral dissertation, York University.

Kasl, S. V. (1980). Epidemiological contributions to the study of work stress. In C. L. Cooper & R. Payne (eds.). *Current concerns in occupational stress* (pp. 3–48). New York: Wiley.

Katz, D., & Kahn, R. (1978). *The social psychology of organizations.* New York: Wiley.

Kennedy, M. M. (1985, July). Burned out on the job: The symptoms, the cure. *Glamour,* p. 82.

Keve, P. W. (1981). *Corrections.* New York: Wiley.

Kim, J., & Mueller, C. W. (1978a). *Introduction to factor analysis: What it is and how to do it.* Beverly Hills, CA: Sage.

____. (1978b). *Factor analysis: Statistical methods and practical issues.* Beverly Hills, CA: Sage.

Klockars, C. B. (1972). A theory of probation supervision. *Journal of Criminal Law, Criminology, and Police Science, 63,* 550–57.

Kobasa, S. C., Maddi, S. R., & Courington, S. (1981). Personality and constitution as mediators in the stress-illness relationship. *Journal of Health and Social Behavior, 22,* 368–78.

Konrad, W. (1986, January). Preventing employee burnout. *Working Woman,* p. 18.

Kramer, M. (1974). *Reality shock: Why nurses leave nursing.* St. Louis: Mosby.

Kroes, W. H., Margolis, B. L., & Hurrell, J. J. (1974). Job stress in policemen. *Journal of Police Science and Administration, 2,* 145–55.

LaRocco, J. M., House, J. S., & French, J. R. P., Jr. (1980). Social support, occupational stress, and health. *Journal of Health and Social Behavior, 21,* 202–18.

Lawler, E. E. (1977). Reward systems. In J. R. Hackman & J. L. Suttle (eds.), *Improving life at work: Behavioral science approaches to organizational change* (pp. 163–226).

Leonard, B. (1982). *Women, crime and society: A critique of theoretical criminology.* New York: Longman.

Lewis-Beck, M. S. (1980). *Applied regression: An introduction.* Beverly Hills, CA: Sage.

Lindquist, C. A., & Whitehead, J. T. (1986a). Burnout, job stress and job satisfaction among Southern correctional officers: Perceptions and causal factors. *Journal of Offender Services, Counseling and Rehabilitation, 10* (4), 5–26.

____. (1986b). Correctional officers as parole officers: An examination of a community supervision sanction. *Criminal Justice and Behavior, 13,* 197–222.

____. (1986c). Guards released from prison: A natural experiment in job enlargement. *Journal of Criminal Justice, 14,* 283–94.

Lipsky, M. (1980). *Street-level bureaucracy.* New York: Russell Sage.

Locke, E. (1976). The nature and causes of job satisfaction. In M. Dunnette (ed.), *Handbook of industrial and organizational psychology* (pp. 1297–349). Chicago: Rand McNally.

Lombardo, L. X. (1981). *Guards imprisoned: Correctional officers at work.* New York: Elsevier.

Long, N., Shouksmith, G., Voges, K., & Roache, S. (1986). Stress in prison staff: An occupational study. *Criminology, 24,* 331–45.

Mahan, S. (1984). Imposition of despair — an ethnography of women in prison. *Justice Quarterly, 1,* 357–83.

Malloy, T. E., & Mays, G. L. (1984). The police stress hypothesis: A critical evaluation. *Criminal Justice and Behavior, 11,* 197–224.

Martin, S. E. (1980). *Breaking and entering: Police women on patrol.* Berkeley, CA: University of California Press.

Martinson, R. (1974). What works? — questions and answers about prison reform. *Public Interest, 35,* 22–54.

Maslach, C. (1976). Burned out. *Human Behavior, 5* (9), 16–22.

____. (1978a). Job burn-out: How people cope. *Public Welfare, 36,* 56–58.

____. (1978b). The client role in staff burn-out. *Journal of Social Issues, 34* (4), 111–24.

____. (1982). *Burnout: The cost of caring.* Englewood Cliffs, NJ: Prentice-Hall.

Maslach, C., & Jackson, S. E. (1978). Lawyer burn-out. *Barrister, 5,* 52–54.

____. (1979). Burned-out cops and their families. *Psychology Today, 12,* 59–62.

____. (1980). The measurement of experienced burnout. Draft of 1981 article.

____. (1981). The measurement of experienced burnout. *Journal of Occupational Behaviour, 2,* 99–113.

____. (1984a). Burnout in organizational settings. In S. Oskamp (ed.), *Applied social psychology annual 5* (pp. 133–53). Beverly Hills, CA: Sage.

____. (1984b). Patterns of burnout among a national sample of public contact workers. *Journal of Health and Human Resources Administration, 7,* 189–212.

Matteson, M. T., & Ivancevich, J. M. (1987). *Controlling work stress: Effective human resource and management strategies.* San Francisco: Jossey-Bass.

McCarthy, B. R. (ed.) (1987). *Intermediate punishments: Intensive supervision, home confinement, and electronic surveillance.* Monsey, NY: Criminal Justice Press.

McCleary, R. (1978). *Dangerous men: The sociology of parole.* Beverly Hills, CA: Sage.

McFadden, R. D. (1982, November 21). City probation services for youth called "inadequate" by civic group. New York *Times,* p. 1.

McGregor, D. (1960). *The human side of enterprise.* New York: McGraw-Hill.

McLean, A. A. (1979). *Work stress.* New York: Addison-Wesley.

McMichael, A. (1978). Personality, behavior, and situational modifiers of work stressors. In C. L. Cooper & R. Payne (eds.), *Stress at work* (pp. 127–47). New York: Wiley.

Miles, A. P. (1965). The reality of the probation officer's dilemma. *Federal Probation, 29*(1), 18–23.

Minahan, A. (1980). Burnout and organizational change. *Social Work, 25,* 87.

Morgan, S. R., & Krehbiel, R. (1985). The psychological condition of burned-out teachers with a nonhumanistic orientation. *Journal of Humanistic Education and Development, 24* (2), 59–67.

National Council on Crime and Delinquency (1981). *Probation and parole directory* (18th ed.). Hackensack, NJ: Author.

National Council on Crime and Delinquency (1987). *The impact of juvenile court sanctions: A court that works: Executive summary.* San Francisco: Author.

Nie, H., Hull, C. H., Jenkins, J. G., Steinbrenner, K., & Bend, D. H. (1975). *SPSS: Statistical package for the social sciences.* New York: McGraw-Hill.

Niederhoffer, A. (1967). *Behind the shield.* Garden City, NY: Doubleday.

Norland, S., & Mann, P. J. (1984). Being troublesome: Women on probation. *Criminal Justice and Behavior, 11,* 115–35.

Ohlin, L. E., Piven, H., & Pappenfort, D. M. (1956). Major dilemmas of the social worker in probation and parole. *National Probation and Parole Officer Journal, 2,* 211–25.

O'Leary, V., & Clear, T. R. (1984). *Directions for community corrections in the 1990s.* Washington, D.C.: National Institute of Corrections.

O'Neill, M., Fransway, L. M., Hanewicz, W. B., Riske, C. R., Edington, D. W., & Carli, T. (1981). *Police occupational stress prevention and job performance: A report of an experiment.* Unpublished report, Michigan State University, East Lansing.

Owen, B. A. (1985). Race and gender relations among prison workers. *Crime and Delinquency, 31,* 147–59.

Paine, W. S. (ed.) (1982). *Job stress and burnout: Research, theory, and intervention perspectives.* Beverly Hills, CA: Sage.

Payne, R. (1980). Organizational stress and social support. In C. L. Cooper & R. Payne (eds.), *Stress at work* (pp. 269–98). New York: Wiley.

Pearlin, L. I., Lieberman, M. A., Menaghan, E. G., & Mullan, J. T. (1981). The stress process. *Journal of Health and Social Behavior, 22,* 337–56.

Perrow, C. (1970). *Organizational analysis: A sociological view.* Monterey, CA: Brooks/Cole.

Perrow, C. (1979). *Complex organizations: A critical essay* (2d ed.). Glenview, IL: Scott, Foresman.

Peters, T. J. (1985). *A passion for excellence: The leadership difference.* New York: Random House.

Peters, T. J., & Waterman, R. H. (1982). *In search of excellence: Lessons from America's best-run companies.* New York: Harper & Row.

Petersilia, J. (1986). Exploring the option of house arrest. *Federal Probation, 50* (2), 50–55.

Petersilia, J., Turner, S., Kahan, J., & Peterson, J. (1985). Executive summary of Rand's study, "Granting felons probation: Public risks and alternatives." *Crime and Delinquency, 31,* 379–92.

Petronio, R. J. (1982). Role socialization of juvenile court probation officers. *Criminal Justice and Behavior, 9,* 143–58.

Philliber, S. (1987). Thy brother's keeper: A review of the literature on correctional officers. *Justice Quarterly, 4,* 9–37.

Pines, A., & Aronson, M. (1981). *From tedium to personal growth.* New York: Free Press.

Pines, A., & Kafry, D. (1978). Occupational tedium in the social services. *Social Work, 23,* 499–507.

Pines, A., & Maslach, C. (1980). Combatting staff burn-out in a day care center: A case study. *Child Care Quarterly, 9,* 5–16.

Polisky, R. J. (1981a). Enhancing the job satisfaction of probation and parole officers. Part I. *Corrections Today, 43* (1), 78–85.

____. (1981b). Enhancing the job satisfaction of probation and parole officers. Part II. *Corrections Today, 43* (2), 54–95.

Potts, L. W. (1983). Female professionals in corrections: Equal employment opportunity issues. *Federal Probation, 37* (1), 37–44.

Pownal, G. A. (1963). An analysis of the role of the parole officer. (Doctoral dissertation, University of Illinois).

Price, B. R., & Skoloff, N. J. (eds.) (1982). *The criminal justice system and women: Women offenders, victims, workers.* New York: Clark Boardman.

Quinn, R., & Staines, G. (1979). *The 1977 quality of employment survey.* Ann Arbor, MI: University of Michigan Survey Research Center.

Remington, P. W. (1981). *Policing: The occupation and the introduction of female officers: An anthropologist's study.* Washington, D.C.: University Press of America.

Rizzo, J. R., House, R., & Lirtzman, S. (1970). Role conflict and ambiguity in complex organizations. *Administrative Science Quarterly, 15,* 150–63.

Robinson, J. P., Athanasiou, R., & Head, K. B. (1978). *Measures of occupational attitudes and occupational characteristics.* Ann Arbor, MI: University of Michigan Survey Research Center.

Rosecrance, J. (1986). Probation supervision: Mission impossible. *Federal Probation, 50* (1), 25–31.

Rubin, H. T. (1985). *Juvenile justice: Policy, practice, and law* (2d ed.). New York: Random House.

Schlacter, P. (1980). Job stress in corrections officers (Doctoral dissertation, The Ohio State University, 1980). *Dissertation Abstracts International, 41,* 4294.

Schmidt, A. K. (1986). Electronic monitors. *Federal Probation, 50* (2), 56–59.

Schoonmaker, M. H., & Brooks, J. S. (1975). Women in probation and parole. *Crime and Delinquency, 21,* 109–15.

Sechrest, L., White, S. O., & Brown, E. D. (eds.) (1979). *The rehabilitation of criminal offenders: Problems and prospects.* Washington, D.C.: National Academy of Sciences.

Selye, H. (1976). *The stress of life* (rev. ed.). New York: McGraw-Hill.

Shamir, B., & Drory, A. (1982). Occupational tedium among prison officers. *Criminal Justice and Behavior, 9,* 79–99.

Shannon, C., & Saleebey, D. (1980). Training child welfare workers to cope with burnout. *Child Welfare, 59,* 463–68.

Shapiro, C. H. (1982). Creative supervision: An underutilized antidote. In W. S. Paine (ed.), *Job stress and burnout: Research, theory, and intervention perspectives* (pp. 213–28). Beverly Hills, CA: Sage.

Shireman, C. H., & Reamer, F. G. (1986). *Rehabilitating juvenile justice.* New York: Columbia University Press.

Shover, N., & Einstadter, W. J. (1988). *Analyzing American corrections.* Belmont, CA: Wadsworth.

Simon, R. J. (1975). *The contemporary woman and crime.* Rockville, MD: National Institute of Mental Health.

Smith, B. L., & Ward, R. S. (1983). Stress on military and civilian police personnel. *American Journal of Police, 3,* 111–26.

Smith, J. O. (1982). Rekindling the flame. *Federal Probation, 46,* 63–66.

Smykla, J. O. (1984). *Probation and parole: Crime control in the community.* New York: Macmillan.

Stanley, D. T. (1976). *Prisoners among us: The problem of parole.* Washington, D.C.: Brookings.

Stout, E. (1973). Women in probation and parole. *Crime and Delinquency, 19,* 62–66.

Street, D., Vinter, R. D., & Perrow, C. (1966). *Organizations for treatment.* New York: Free Press.

Studt, E. (1973). *Surveillance and service in parole: A report of the parole action study.* Washington, D.C.: National Institute of Corrections.

Sullivan, D. C., Elwin, E., & Dexter, T. (1977). *Probation as a workplace: A qualitative analysis of the job of a probation officer.* Albany, NY: New York State Division of Probation.

Sykes, G. (1958). *The society of captives: A study of a maximum security prison.* Princeton, NJ: Princeton University Press.

Thomson, D. R. (1987). The changing face of probation in the USA. In J. K. Harding (ed.), *Probation in the community: A policy and practice reader.* London: Tavistock.

Thomson, D., & Fogel, D. (1980). *Probation work in small agencies: A national study of training provisions and needs.* Chicago: University of Illinois at Chicago Circle Center for Research in Criminal Justice.

Toch, H. (1979). Alienation as a vehicle of change. *Journal of Community Psychology, 7,* 3–11.

Toch, H., & Grant, J. D. (1975). *Agents of change: A study in police reform.* New York: Wiley.

Toch, H., & Klofas, J. (1982). Alienation and desire for job enrichment among correction officers. *Federal Probation, 46* (1), 35–44.

Tomaino, L. (1975). The five faces of probation. *Federal Probation, 39* (4), 42–45.

Townsey, R. D. (1982). Black women in American policing: An advancement display. *Journal of Criminal Justice, 10*, 455–68,

Travis, L. F. (1985). *Probation, parole, and community corrections: A reader.* Prospect Heights, IL: Waveland.

Trester, H. B. (1981). *Supervision of the offender.* Englewood Cliffs, NJ: Prentice-Hall.

Ursprung, A. W. (1986). Burnout in the human services: A review of the literature. *Rehabilitation Counseling Bulletin,* 190–99.

Van Deusen, J., Yarbrough, J., & Cornelsen, D. (1985). Short-term system-therapy with adult probation clients and their families. *Federal Probation, 49* (4), 21–26.

Vash, C. L. (1980). *The burnt-out administrator.* New York: Springer.

Vito, G. F. (1986). Felony probation and recidivism: Replication and response. *Federal Probation, 50* (4), 17–25.

von Hirsch, A. (1984, January). Selective incapacitation: A critique. *National Institute of Justice Reports,* pp. 5–8.

Vroom, V. (1959). Some personality determinants of the effects of participation. *Journal of Abnormal and Social Psychology, 59*, 322–27.

____. (1964). *Work and motivation.* New York: Wiley.

Waller, I. (1974). *Men released from prison.* Toronto: University of Toronto Press.

Walsh, A. (1984). Gender-based differences: A study of probation officers' attitudes about, and recommendations for, felony sexual assault cases. *Criminology, 22*, 371–87.

Weisheit, R. A. (1984). Female homicide offenders: Trends over time in an institutionalized population. *Justice Quarterly, 1*, 471–89.

Wexler, J., & Logan, D. (1983). Sources of stress among women police officers. *Journal of Police Science and Administration, 11*, 46–53.

Whitehead, J. T. (1985). Job burnout in probation and parole: Its extent and intervention implications. *Criminal Justice and Behavior, 12*, 91–110.

____. (1986a). Gender differences in probation: A case of no differences. *Justice Quarterly, 3,* 51–65.

____. (1986b). Job burnout and job satisfaction among probation managers. *Journal of Criminal Justice, 14,* 25–35.

____. (1987). Probation officer job burnout: A test of two theories. *Journal of Criminal Justice, 15,* 1–16.

Whitehead, J. T., & Lindquist, C. A. (1985). Job stress and burnout among probation/parole officers: Perceptions and causal factors. *International Journal of Offender Therapy and Comparative Criminology, 29,* 109–19.

____. (1986). Correctional officer job burnout: A path model. *Journal of Research in Crime and Delinquency, 23,* 23–42.

____. (1987). Intensive supervision: Officer perspectives. In B. R. McCarthy (ed.), *Intermediate punishments: Intensive supervision, home confinement, and electronic surveillance* (pp. 67–84). Monsey, NY: Criminal Justice Press.

Wilson, N. K. (1981). The masculinity of violent crime — some second thoughts. *Journal of Criminal Justice, 9,* 111–23.

Wolfe, N. T., Cullen, F. T., & Cullen, J. B. (1984). Describing the female offender: A note on the demographics of arrests. *Journal of Criminal Justice, 12,* 483–92.

Wooten, H. B. (1985). It's o.k., supervision enthusiasts: You can come home now. *Federal Probation, 49* (4), 4–7.

Yates, J. E. (1979). *Managing stress: A businessperson's guide.* New York: Amacrom.

Yuenger, J. (1981, February 1). Teacher burnout — our classroom crisis. Chicago *Tribune,* pp. 1 & 10.

Zimmer, L. E. (1986). *Women guarding men.* Chicago: University of Chicago Press.

Index

About the Author

JOHN T. WHITEHEAD is an assistant professor at East Tennessee State University. Before this position, he taught at the University of Alabama at Birmingham and was a probation officer in Buffalo, New York. Dr. Whitehead has published in the areas of job burnout, correctional officer professional orientation, and the effectiveness of correctional treatment. His articles have appeared in *Criminal Justice and Behavior, Crime and Delinquency,* the *Journal of Criminal Justice, Justice Quarterly,* and the *Journal of Research in Crime and Delinquency.* He is completing a text on juvenile justice with Steven P. Lab.